GUIDE TO LIFE

By the same author

The Experience of Depression (1978) reissued as
Choosing Not Losing (1988)

The Construction of Life and Death (1982) reissued as
The Courage to Live (1991)

Depression: The Way Out of Your Prison (1983)

Living with the Bomb: Can We Live without Enemies? (1985)

Beyond Fear (1987)

The Successful Self (1988)

The Depression Handbook (1990) reissued as
Breaking the Bonds (1991)

Wanting Everything (1991)

Time on Our Side (1994)

GUIDE TO LIFE

DOROTHY ROWE

HarperCollins*Publishers*

HarperCollins*Publishers*
77–85 Fulham Palace Road,
Hammersmith, London W6 8JB

Published by HarperCollins*Publishers* 1995
1 3 5 7 9 8 6 4 2

ISBN 0 00 255562 X

Set in Linotron Galliard by
Rowland Phototypesetting Ltd, Bury St Edmunds, Suffolk

Printed in Great Britain by
HarperCollinsManufacturing Glasgow

CONTENTS

To my publisher and friend
Mike Fishwick

Some five hundred years before the birth of Christ the Greek poet Xenophanes wrote,

The gods did not reveal, from the beginning,
All things to us; but in the course of time,
Through seeking we may learn, and know things better.
But as for certain truth, no man has known it,
Nor will he know it; neither of the gods,
Nor yet of the things of which I speak.
And even if by chance he were to utter
The final truth, he would himself not know it;
For all is but a woven web of guesses.[1]

Albert Einstein wrote,

As far as the laws of mathematics refer to reality, they are not certain; and as far as they are certain, they do not refer to reality.[2]

Life is simple, but only if you understand what life is and what you are.

Alas, many people don't understand what life and they are about. So they struggle blindly through life, being hurt and hurting others, feeling confused and frightened but not knowing why. Because they don't understand themselves, they cannot change, and, indeed, they believe that they cannot change. They think that life is just as they see it.

Yet, all we need to know to understand life and ourselves is very simple.

It's something that everyone knows, but not everyone knows that they know it.

Life is simple, but only if you understand what life is and what you are.

Alas, many people don't understand what life and they are about. So they struggle blindly through life, being hurt and hurting others, feeling confused and frightened but not knowing why. Because they don't understand themselves, they cannot change, and, indeed, they believe that they cannot change. They think that life is just as they see it.

Yet, all we need to know to understand life and ourselves is very simple.

It's something that everyone knows, but not everyone knows that they know it.

CONTENTS

To my publisher and friend
Mike Fishwick

CHAPTER 1

The Secret of Life

THE SECRET of life is that there is no secret.

All that you need to know about life is there for you to see. All you have to do is open your eyes and recognize what you already know.

However, down the centuries, many people wanting power have tried to keep the secret secret. They have created their theories and their jargon, and told us that they and they alone know the secret of life. These are the people who have claimed to be the wisest of the wise. They have called themselves philosophers, theologians, clergy, doctors, psychiatrists, psychologists, psychotherapists, counsellors – in short, experts on life and living. Jungians say we are all part of the collective unconscious, while psychiatrists say that we are the product of our genes. Each of these theories is a way of describing and explaining certain parts of human experience, but no one theory can describe, let alone explain it all.

Some of these people have always known that there is no secret, while others have insisted that they and they alone know the Secret Truth About Life.

Down the centuries a few of these experts have dared to reveal that there is no secret, and, consequently, have been reviled by their colleagues. How dare such renegades say that each of us can sort things out for ourselves! How dare they threaten the experts' power, prestige and wealth!

The experts always protect themselves by forming themselves into an elite and guarding the entrance with a formidable barrier of examinations and rituals through which only a chosen few can pass.

When the selected few do get through the barrier they are faced with a choice. Do you now tell yourself that you are initiated into the Secret Truth About Life? Or do you bear the disappointment of your discovery that what you might have is simply a collection of useful research results (for instance, we now know that babies are born with the ability to distinguish faces from all other phenomena) and, if you look for it, the kind of wisdom in living which has always been available to every generation.

Amongst the experts this wisdom has been more known than used. On the whole, the personal lives of experts are far from edifying. Some experts do live wisely but most (I'm speaking from years of observation) manage their lives no better than the rest of us. They've been so busy being experts they haven't learnt what they need to know.

The secret which is no secret is that there is a body of knowledge which concerns how to live wisely. This wisdom is available to all of us. You don't need a brilliant intelligence and a superb education to understand it, absorb it and use it.

However, just as we are all born artists, musicians, mathematicians and explorers and our upbringing and education take most of these abilities away from us, so we are born with the ability to understand ourselves and life, and the adults around us pour scorn on this ability and forbid us to use it. In learning to be good, obedient members of society we lose touch with the knowledge we need if we are to live our lives in ways which are rich and fulfilling.

A rich and fulfilling life is not one of unalloyed happiness. No amount of wisdom can defend us from loss, disappointment, old age and death, nor from the idiocies committed by those who have political and economic power.

However, such wisdom does ensure that we can live comfortably with ourselves and with other people. Being comfortable with yourself means that you are not forever thinking about and worrying about yourself, always prey to difficult and unpleasant emotions. Being comfortable with other people means that you are not afraid of others but can enjoy their company. There's no longer a barrier between you and other people. No longer

burdened with the sense of your own inadequacies, you cease to see the world as a cold, evil, disappointing place and instead become aware of the world's infinite possibilities.

What follows here is not a list of Absolute Truths. The way we are physically constituted means that if there are any Absolute Truths in the universe we could not recognize one even if we stumbled over it. What we have are relative truths, conclusions we have drawn from our experience and which are always relative to our past experience and the situation in which we find ourselves.

We each have our own relative truths, and if we compare notes we can see that some of us have arrived at much the same relative truths. This suggests that perhaps we have managed to approximate that kind of relative truth which, in a random universe, turns up fairly frequently. We can then decide, if we were laying a bet, on which of these truths we would put our money.

Writing this kind of book creates for me the problem of which of the personal pronouns I should use. Should I say 'them' or 'us', 'me' or 'you'?

Using 'they' and 'them' puts a distance between them and us (my reader and me) and sometimes I want to do this.

I use 'we' and 'us' when I'm talking about something which everybody is likely to do at some time or other.

I use 'I' and 'me' when I'm talking about some part of my own experience which may or may not be like that of other people.

When I use 'you' and 'your' I don't mean that you, my dear reader, have had all the experiences or think in all the different ways which I am describing. No person could live so long or be so changeable. I am simply assuming that with some of my anecdotes about 'you' you will feel an identity. Others of these anecdotes are an invitation for you to make a leap of imagination into someone else's world. 'Ah, yes,' you might think, 'that reminds me of so-and-so. Is that what he thinks? I wonder.'

Understanding yourself and understanding other people are exactly the same process.

CHAPTER 2

Life – What You Can't Change and What You Can

WHEN YOU think about your life, do you feel that you are as you are, the world is as you see it, your past was what it was, your present is what it is, and your future will be very much what you expect it to be?

Do you feel that although some parts of you, your life and the world can change, you, your life and the world are, in essence, fixed?

Do you feel that you are as you are, your life is what it is, and the world is what it is?

Do you feel that in knowing yourself, your life and the world, you know what reality is?

Do you feel that you, your life and the world are your fixed, unalterable fate? They are as they are, and they are your lot. They are reality.

If this is what you feel, then you are mistaken.

You, your life and the world are not fixed, unalterable parts of reality which you have to put up with and cope with as best you can. What you see as being you, your life and the world is not reality. You, your life and the world are matters that you can change.

What you see as you, your life and the world are the set of conclusions you have drawn from your experience of life which began when you were a tiny babe tucked in your mum's womb and your growing brain, like the hardware in a computer, got to the stage where it could run your software, commonly called your mind or, less commonly, your 'meaning structure'.

To describe what I mean by a meaning structure I have used the analogy of a computer, but this is quite inadequate because our brains can do much more than the most advanced computer can.

A computer's hardware is built and then the software, which someone has constructed separately, is fed into it, whereas the hardware and the software of a brain develop together. Our brains come equipped with much more than what can be observed when a brain is dissected or scanned.

Our brains come equipped with tools which are there as potentialities until our interaction with the environment brings that potential into use. Thus before the potential of your tool of language could come into being and be used you had to have a language spoken around you and you had to be able to hear it.

Clever though these tools are, their function is not to reveal reality to you. They are not transparent windows on to the world. Instead, the tool's function is to create a construction which represents some aspect of your experience. This construction is a meaning. If the language you learn to speak is English you'll see the world in the way English creates it. If you learnt Latin or Spanish or Italian or were born in the West Indies you'll see the world differently.

A study of the derivation of words will show just how diversely different languages 'see' the world. The word 'dawn' comes from the Old English *daeg*, 'day', and *dagian*, 'to become light'.[3] Ancient Romans saw dawns where 'the air grows golden', hence *aurora* from *aurum*, gold. Spaniards and Italians saw a white dawn, *alba*, 'the white'. Out of African languages dawn in the West Indies became 'day clean' and cock crow 'Gi me trousers'.[4]

When, shortly after birth, your eyes open, you seem to be surrounded by a blur of events. Then one of your tools comes into operation – the tool of contrast. With this tool some parts of the blur look different from other parts. You start to see patterns. For the rest of your life you will continue to see patterns, even where no patterns actually exist. You'll hear patterns and learn to call the clearly structured patterns you hear 'language' or 'music' and the less clearly structured 'noise'. You'll also learn to feel patterns, taste patterns and smell patterns.

Within a day or so one of these patterns which you see becomes very significant though as yet you don't know why. Your tool of face recognition has come into operation and a few days later you know, though you haven't the words to say it, 'That's my mum.'

Aren't you clever? That's because

The function of your brain is to create meaning.

You could ask, 'Isn't the function of the brain to keep the body alive?'

I would say, 'This is the meaning for the brain which many people now use because this meaning seems to give useful results. But it's only recently in human history that the brain has been given this meaning. In other times and cultures other organs of the body – the heart, the stomach and the bowels – have been given the meaning of being the most important organ. Current research on genes and DNA suggest that it's our genes that have the primary importance. No doubt there are genes which enable our brain to create meaning.'

At the moment of conception the brain starts developing and at some point (current research suggests at about 18 weeks' gestation) meaning starts to be created.

Note that I did not say, 'You start creating meaning.'

There is no YOU sitting inside your brain creating meaning.

Or at least I hope there isn't, because then I'd have to work out how little you-inside-your-brain creates meaning and if little you has a littler you inside and so on and so on to an infinity of you's.

So let's stick with your brain creating meaning.

Now I'm going to abandon the computer metaphor and turn to Lego.

For those of you bereft of children I shall explain that Lego is a toy made up of plastic blocks of all shapes and sizes but all with a regular pattern of circular indentations and raised rings. The rings on one block fit into the indentations of another, thus allowing all sorts of structures to be built. However, if you imagine your brain being made of blocks of Lego the difference would be that this brain Lego is infinitely flexible so that every part can be attached simultaneously to every other and can re-form itself to accommodate any new part that arrives on the scene.

This happens often, because your Lego/brain has many tools which, sometimes working together and sometimes working alone, create new pieces of Lego. Each piece of Lego is a meaning.

Your first piece of Lego/meaning, formed at some point after conception, probably had to do with pleasure and pain. Soon would follow Lego/meanings to do with sounds and pressure, and these would all link together. Ease of pressure would link to pleasure, harsh sounds to pain.

The linked pieces of Lego/meaning form a structure, hence the term *meaning structure*. This meaning structure constantly accommodates new pieces of Lego/meaning and reforms itself in the process. Encountering the outside world brings a constant, never-ending influx of changes, and at some point the meaning structure starts to call itself 'I'.

You are your meaning structure. Your meaning structure is you.

If you like you don't have to think of yourself as a set of flexible Lego. Perhaps you could think of another metaphor. A cell dividing and enlarging, with each new cell being a meaning, is another image I sometimes use.

One of our greatest problems is that the only way we can make sense of anything is in terms of our current meaning structure. We understand something new by seeing it as being like something we already know about. Whenever we encounter something which actually is so new to us that there is nothing in our meaning structure like it we find it hard to make sense of it. This is why keeping up with modern physics is so difficult. It is hard to imagine images like black holes and alternative universes, and even these images are likely to be quite inadequate

in describing what is actually out there because the physicists have to rely on using images that already exist.

I use the Lego image as a way of explaining, first, that what all of us do all the time is to create meaning, and, second, that these meanings hang together and add up to an understanding of what we/our life/the world is.

The fact that you are in essence a meaning-creating creature is what you are stuck with and cannot change.

You cannot change the basic physical constituents of your body.

You cannot grow wings and fly.

You are a non-flying creature but you are a meaning-creating creature.

Your brain/hardware can grow, or suffer injury and decay, and your meaning structure constantly changes, but they are the constituents of your being and you cannot leave them.

You can imagine leaving your body, but this is just one of the amazing tricks your meaning structure can play.

Your meaning structure cannot show you what reality is. All your meaning structure can show you are your own pictures which represent what you think reality is. These pictures are actually inside your head, but your amazing brain and meaning structure persuade you that you are inside the pictures and that what you picture is real.

Presumably some kind of reality outside ourselves exists.

Some philosophers have argued that all that exists are our thoughts, but that seems nonsensical. Am I just imagining the paper I am writing on and you just imagining the book you're reading? I'm sure that if you and I had simply imagined the universe and everything in it we wouldn't have created the terrible things that happen in the world.

The evidence from our experience does seem to point to the existence of reality, the sum total of everything that exists. What this everything is is something we human beings can never know directly. We can only know it indirectly through careful judgement and thought.

Physicists talk about everything that exists as being made up of tiny particles which they give curious names like neutrino, charm, and quark. To large parts of everything that exists they give names like galaxy, nebula, solar systems and black holes.

They talk about these things as if they are reality, but when pressed physicists will explain they cannot possibly see reality.

Erwin Schrodinger wrote,

> The world is a construct of our sensations, perceptions, memories. It is convenient to regard it as existing objectively on its own. But it certainly does not become manifest by its mere existence. Its becoming manifest is conditional on very special goings-on in very special parts of this world, namely on certain events that happen in a brain.[5]

We all make different kinds of observations, but these observations depend on where we are and what we expect to see. What we see and report is not reality but our interpretation of reality.

This is all that any of us can do.

We can never know reality directly.

All we can ever know are our interpretations of reality.

What you know as you, your life and the world is not reality. What you know as you, yourself and the world is your interpretation of you, your life and the world.

Seeing, hearing, touching, smelling, tasting are always, even at their very simplest, interpretations, just as intuitions are interpretations.

Interpretations are meanings.

We are always in the business of creating meanings.

This is what you cannot change.

You cannot *not* create meaning.

Imagine you're sitting quietly in your room and something happens. Your awareness of this happening *is* your interpretation. The beginning of your interpretation, entirely without words, is, say, 'a very loud sound'. Immediately, before you stir from your seat to find out why the loud sound occurred, you give the sound a meaning. You might think it was an explosion, or a car crash, or a breaking window and so on. After interpreting the sound you might decide to check whether you were right.

You don't have to be conscious to create meaning.

Even fast asleep, you interpret a happening as being in your body and you move to release your trapped arm, all without you waking.

It is our interpretations which determine how we think, feel and act. Thus,

It's not what happens to you that matters but how you interpret what happens to you.

You ALWAYS have a choice about how you will interpret what happens to you.

This applies even in the most extreme situations.

Suppose you are told that you have a particularly nasty form of cancer. How will you interpret this?

Some alternative interpretations are:

I won't let this beat me.
This is the end.
This is God's punishment for my wickedness.
If I'm a good patient the doctors will save me.
Conventional medicine is useless.

And so on.

Anyone who says, 'There is no alternative' has merely rejected all other choices.

Interpretations are choices.

A friend who had had a Catholic upbringing and so saw herself, her life and her world as an unchangeable part of the Absolute, Eternal Truths of the Catholic Church told me that the best thing she got from therapy was learning that she had choices.

You can always change your choice.

You might initially interpret your illness as, 'This is God's punishment for my wickedness' but later think, 'That's silly' and decide upon, 'I won't let this beat me.'

Having made one interpretation you then interpret your interpretation.

Interpreting your illness as God's punishment might lead you to further interpretations such as, 'I deserve this punishment,' or, 'I must be good and accept my punishment and not do anything to get better.' Deciding that your illness is a challenge to be mastered might lead you to interpret this as, 'I'll do everything I can to get better,' or, 'I'll get on with my life as normal.'

Life has many paradoxes.

A paradox is not a problem.

A problem is a question which, in theory at least, is capable of being answered.

A paradox is a seeming contradiction which nevertheless contains an element of a truth.

A PARADOX OF LIFE

Even though we can never know reality directly, to survive and flourish we must always strive to make interpretations that are as close to reality as possible.

For instance, suppose you're about to cross a busy road. You can't possibly know the exact speed of approaching traffic, but to cross the road safely you must judge the speed of the traffic as accurately as possible. How do you make this judgement?

Suppose a friend who is a very successful stockbroker advises you to put your savings in shares that, he says, are sure to increase in value. How do you judge the likelihood that what he says is true?

We create new interpretations out of the interpretations we have already acquired. We have nothing else to use. We might decide not to bother with sorting through these old interpretations to create something new and just run out on to the road or impulsively give our money to the stockbroker. Or we might think carefully about our past experiences, contrasting one with another, and compare our past interpretations with our present observations to be as sure as we can that our new interpretation is as good an interpretation of reality as it can be. We can compare the speeds of a number of passing cars, or do some research about current stock prices.

Although we might know about many alternative ways of interpreting some aspect of reality, we each can have our own favourite way of interpreting that aspect.

However, our favourite ways of creating our interpretations can result in interpretations which are far from reality.

For instance, we all know that envelopes come in many sizes and colours. Some people, however, when inspecting their mail, see and open white and coloured envelopes but never see, much less open brown envelopes. Yet unpaid bills don't disappear into thin air.

We need to be aware how one group of our wishes can dominate all our interpretations. We can choose to see only what we wish to see and thus do only what we wish to do. However, our wishes might not be an accurate reflection of reality, particularly that part of reality which is composed of other people's interpretations. We forget that other people see things differently from us.

You must have noticed that no two people ever interpret an event in exactly the same way. You interpret a television programme as being excellent. Your friend thinks it's rubbish. This is not a matter of other people being mad, bad or awkward. It is an inescapable part of the way we are physically constituted.

Each of us, every moment of our lives, asleep or awake, is engaged in interpreting what is happening.

Each of us has only one source we can draw on in creating our interpretations.

This is our past experience.

No two people ever have the same past experience.

Identical twins might begin life with the same genetic components, but life in the womb differs for each of them, one is born after the other and from the moment they are born they have different experiences.

To the extent that two people create similar interpretations they can communicate, but even when two people speak the same language they create very different interpretations. Thus two people can live side by side, speak the same language, yet each interpret the world in totally different ways. It's often said, for instance, that men and women inhabit different planets!

So here we are, each of us in our own little world of interpretations, yet, at the same time, we are born social animals.

We are physically constituted as social animals.

When you were born you didn't just search around for a food-bearing nipple. You also searched for a friendly face. You were born knowing how to recognize a face and preferring to look at a face than at anything else.

If a friendly face hadn't turned up for you to talk to, you wouldn't be reading this now. Without a friendly face, even if you'd been adequately fed and kept warm, you would have either died in the first few weeks (it's a condition known as 'anaclitic depression') or you would have gone on to become one of those strange individuals who are unable to see other people as being in any way different from other objects.

Out of the bond we develop with a mothering person in our own first months of life grows our sense of right and wrong, guilt and reparation. Babies who don't get the chance to develop this bond grow up to be conscienceless people. They might lead apparently quite ordinary lives, whether criminals or company directors, but their personal relationships are always a disaster.

A PARADOX OF LIFE

We are each a unique individual living in our own individual, self-created world, yet we need one another in order to survive.

The interpretations we create don't just exist on their own. They arise out of the set of interpretations we have created in the past and they also determine how we think, feel and act.

Whatever we think, feel and do has endless consequences.

This is another aspect of life which we cannot change.

It has to do with the nature of reality.

Whatever reality is, it does seem that it is a vast, ever-changing interconnectedness. Everything is constantly moving and everything is connected to everything else. Physicists say this, and so did the ancient Hindu, Taoist and Buddhist philosophers.

Because everything is connected to everything else,

All our acts have consequences.

Don't kid yourself that what you do will have no consequences, or very limited consequences, or that you can decide what the consequences will be. A father might say, 'I caught my son stealing. I gave him a good hiding and that was the end of it', but he is deluding himself. The father's actions will have consequences beyond the father's control as a result of how the son interprets what his father has done.

Everything you do has consequences and these consequences spread in all directions and go on forever.

A PARADOX OF LIFE

Everything that happens has good consequences and bad consequences.

For instance, you win the lottery.

Good consequences: You give up working and plan a round-the-world luxury voyage.

Bad consequences: Your entire family comes too.

Remember that 'good' and 'bad' are not Absolute and Eternal Judgements existing outside our human life. We each have our own interpretation of good and bad. Some people believe that lotteries are wicked. Some people wouldn't want to go anywhere without their family.

A PARADOX OF LIFE

Every interpretation we can create has good and bad implications.

Suppose your interpretation of the right way to behave includes the belief that you will always tell the truth.

The good implication of this is that people always know

where they are with you, and the bad implication is that people are sometimes hurt by what you say.

Because every interpretation has good implications and bad implications, and every action has good consequences and bad consequences, life can never be perfect.

The longing for perfection is the longing for an illusion.

If you want to be miserable, *believe that you and the world ought to be perfect.*

You will always feel guilty, angry and disappointed.

If you want to be miserable, *don't try to make your interpretations as close to reality as possible.*

You will always feel surprised, confused and fearful.

If you want to be miserable, *believe that you, your life and the world are reality, fixtures which you cannot change.*

You will always feel trapped and hopeless.

If you are miserable and want to change, say to yourself,

'The way I interpret myself, my life and my world has implications and consequences which make me miserable.

What alternative interpretations can I discover for what has happened, is happening and will happen to me?

Which of these interpretations will give me the most satisfaction and happiness?'

Let's look at the important components of 'myself', 'my life' and my world'.

CHAPTER 3

You and Your Own Truth

IF I WERE to ask you, 'What kind of a person are you?' and you were to answer truthfully, would you say,

'Other people looking at me think that I'm a very together person, that I'm competent and confident, get on well with other people, always cheerful, kind – but they don't know the real me. Underneath I'm very different. I'm not as confident and competent as I make out, and I'm not a nice person at all. I try not to let people know me as I am.'

If I asked you, 'If you were a house, how would you describe yourself?' would you say,

'As a house I've got lots of rooms that represent different parts of me. On the outside the house looks all right – could be better but it will pass. There's a front door that's always closed. I'll let a few people into the front rooms. They're cheerful, nicely furnished rooms, good for work and socializing. There's a room behind the front rooms where I let only one or two people in. It's a rather sombre room. That's where I am when I'm not with people. Beneath that room there's a cellar. I keep the door to the cellar locked. There's something terrible in that cellar. If people knew about what's at the centre of my house that would be the end of me.'

Most people experience their existence as being something like this house.

Some people try to pretend that their cellar and its terrible contents don't exist. This pretence leaves them feeling that they don't have a whole house, just a facade of a house. They feel that they aren't a person, just a facade of a person. They spend their time in their front room socializing and being good and kind to people. They need to be busy and have lots of excitement to stop them being aware of the emptiness and darkness lurking inside themselves.

Other people are always aware of the danger in the cellar. They believe that the only way to keep the cellar locked and hidden is for them to be very good. If they're a good son/daughter, wife/husband, father/mother, employer/employee, friend and citizen they can keep the evil danger inside them well locked away. This is a never-ending task and their vigilance must be constant.

Most people believe that they are, in essence, bad and unacceptable, but that if they keep this essence hidden, and if they work hard to be good, other people won't discover how bad they are and they'll be accepted, and even liked and loved.

Most people believe that this is how they are, and that this is fixed and unchangeable.

If this is what you believe, then you are mistaken.

When you were born you didn't experience yourself as being bad and unacceptable. When you were born you/your house was open-plan and everyone was invited in. You didn't know anything about cellars and dangerous, dark forces inside you. You were as you were, open, curious, trusting, wanting to love and be loved, to please and be pleased.

Then the people around you, the very ones you wanted to please so they would love you, began suggesting that there was something nasty inside you and that your open-plan house needed a cellar where this nastiness could be locked away. This nastiness had names. There was greed ('Babies should be fed at regular intervals and not just when they want to be fed'), dirtiness ('You've soiled yourself. You're disgusting'), selfishness ('Wait your turn'), aggression ('You're a wicked child to hit your sister').

All the time you were interpreting what was happening to you.

(You developed the ability to create meaning while you were still in the womb. We begin creating interpretations long before we have a language in which to describe these interpretations. Our interpretations take the form of feelings, images and sounds. Studies of babies in the womb show that they prefer the sweet melodies of Mozart to the taut sharpness of Stravinsky. No doubt once born they can distinguish the sound of 'Dearest darling' from the sound of 'You filthy pig' even though they don't know the meaning of the words.)

Like everyone else, the only way you could create your interpretations was to use your past experience. But you were a tiny child. You didn't have much experience but you did try to create the very best interpretations that you possibly could. You interpreted events and drew conclusions from your interpretations.

You found the world to be a very confusing place. Fortunately your mother explained the world to you.

There you were, toddling along on unsteady feet and your mother said, 'Be careful or you'll fall and hurt yourself.'

You took no notice. Then you fell over and hurt yourself. You drew a conclusion from this. You thought, 'My mum knows what's what. She tells me the truth.'

Soon after you had another accident. Perhaps you wet yourself or knocked over a glass of milk. Your mother said, 'You disgusting, wicked child. You'll be the death of me' (or words to that effect).

Using your past experience you interpreted what she said.

You had found out that your mother knows the world and tells the truth. (You had no idea that she'd quarrelled with your father and was taking her bad feelings out on you.)

For you the truth now is that you disgust your mother and you are so wicked that you will kill her with your wickedness.

This dangerous, disgusting wickedness is inside you.

And so your open-plan house acquires an inner room.

You know now that this inner room can get you into trouble. And so it does.

You find yourself in a situation from which you cannot escape and in which an adult whom you rely on is inflicting pain on you.

Perhaps it's your mother or father, who love you and only

want 'the best' for you. They want you to be clean and toilet-trained. They want you to do as you're told, to be a sweet, pleasant, good child, a credit to them as parents. So they punish you when you're not.

Perhaps your parents have abandoned you. Perhaps they don't want you, or perhaps they're doing the best they can for you but have to earn a living. Perhaps they're ill, or dead.

Perhaps an adult is beating you, or using you in strange and painful ways.

Whatever the situation, it is for you the extremes of pain and danger.

You interpret the situation as, 'I am being punished by my *bad* parent.'

Then you remember that you depend on this bad parent and you feel even more frightened.

What can you do?

You can do what we all do when we are in a situation from which we cannot escape and which is causing us pain.

We can change how we interpret the situation.

This is what you do.

You remember that dark room in your self/house. You realize that it is your fault that you are suffering. Your interpretation of the situation now becomes, 'I am bad and am being punished by my good parent.'

Now you are safe in the care of your *good* parent.

Now your house has a cellar that contains something dark and dangerous and which you must keep hidden.

Now you can never just be yourself.

Now you know you must be good. Soon you are an expert in being good.

Some unlucky children do more than just learn how to be good. Perhaps this happened to you. Perhaps instead of that extreme situation occurring just a few times in your early child-hood it occurred again and again. The adult you relied on kept inflicting pain on you.

How could you keep telling yourself that this adult was good and you deserved this punishment?

By re-interpreting your interpretation.

You decide that, 'I am bad and am being punished by my good parent, and when I grow up I shall punish bad people in the way I was punished.'

Now you have learnt how to be cruel. Now when you grow up you'll be able to say, 'I was beaten as a child and it never did me any harm.' What you don't realize is that the harm the beatings have done is to let you think that you haven't suffered any harm.

The harm that you have suffered is that you no longer know what your own truth is.

You think that your dark cellar contains something wicked and dangerous. You don't know that it contains nothing dangerous at all. What is hidden in there is something you came into the world knowing, something the adults around you have forbidden you to know: your own truth.

Once you know something you can't unknow it. So, to survive you had to hide your knowledge. This is what you did.

When you were small you didn't need me to explain to you that each of us has our own way of seeing things. You knew that. You were often surprised that other people didn't see things in the same way as you. You'd say, 'Oh yes' to something, and your parents would say, 'Oh no.' But that was one of the things which you found interesting.

You knew that you saw things in your way. You had your own truth.

Then the adults took that knowledge away from you.

The first time that happened was perhaps something like this. You were just big and strong enough to take a loose lid off a jar. Inside was something white which oozed when you squeezed it. If you moved your hand it spread itself across the carpet in a very interesting way, and if you bounced your hand against the carpet bits of it flew off and formed a pretty pattern. You were busy being a scientist and an artist. This was exciting. This was marvellous.

Then your mother arrived.

You recognized that she did not see the situation in the same way as you did.

If you were lucky she reacted calmly. Perhaps she said, 'I

know you're enjoying yourself and that you're learning a lot, but I'd rather you did that with soapsuds instead of my expensive face cream. I have my way of seeing things and on this occasion my view is going to prevail. Let's get you and the room cleaned up.'

Most of us weren't that lucky. Most of us were left in no doubt that our mother saw the situation differently. What she did was to show us that our way of seeing the situation was utterly, utterly wrong while her way was right and that we were very bad.

Bringing up children isn't easy. Children do have to be told that many of their interpretations are not a good reflection of the situation and thus likely to lead to danger. Many a child has thought that the red circle on top of the stove would be nice to touch. But parents have a choice of how to tell the child this isn't so.

(1) Parents can concentrate on the child's interpretation of the event and, arising out of this interpretation, what the child did.

For instance, a parent restraining a child from running across a busy road can say, 'The cars are moving faster than you think. Wait until the road is clear.'

OR

(2) Parents can ignore how the child has interpreted an event and simply tell the child that he is silly, stupid, childish, wicked to do what he did.

They can say, 'You wicked child. How many times have I told you not to run across the road!'

(1) draws the child's attention to the interpretation he has created and suggests that he can create a better interpretation and thus act more effectively.

(2) tells the child that there is something intrinsically wrong with him.

However,

(1) requires the parent to think, be creative, be patient and to ignore those adults who are watching and thinking, even saying, 'If that was my child I'd give him a good hiding.'

Whereas

(2) is quick and can be a self-satisfying expression of the parent's anger arising from his or her anxiety about the child.

On the whole, parents are more expert in interpreting the world than are children. However, there is one part of the world where the child, not the parent, is the expert.

The child is the expert in knowing about his own thoughts and feelings. The child knows what these are. The parent can only guess.

This applies to all of us.

When I say, 'We can never know reality directly,' I mean the reality of what goes on around us. There is one aspect of reality we do know directly and that is our inner world of thoughts and feelings. In judging the world around us, however carefully, we can only make approximations; we can never enter and know another person's inner world, but we always know directly and accurately what we think and feel and why. We know our own truth.

Unfortunately, most of us don't know that we know. We had that knowledge taken away from us when we were children.

Some parents take our knowledge away accidentally out of exasperation. Imagine the kind of scene where the child is making those unpleasant sounds which Australians call 'grizzling'. The child feels in need of a cuddle and something to eat. He says, 'I'm hungry. I want a biscuit.' His mother says, 'You're not hungry. You're tired. Go to bed.'

The child is confused. He thought his feelings meant he was hungry but his mother says this isn't so. She implies that she knows his feelings better than he does.

Our own truth is always private. Other people cannot know our truth unless we choose to tell them.

Small children have to learn that this is so. Some parents lie to their children in order to make them obedient. They say to the child, 'I know what you're thinking.'

Sometimes the parent is right about what the child is thinking. It's an educated guess, not direct knowledge, but the child doesn't know that her parent is making a guess from an assessment of the situation and the expression on the child's face. The child thinks that the parent can read her mind.

I've met many adults who still have the feeling that their

parents can read their minds. They dare not think, much less say, anything critical about their parents in case the parent, however far distant, knows what they are thinking and punishes them by making them feel guilty. 'How could you think that, after all I've done for you.'

I've come across many people who, seeing psychologists as parental figures, believe that psychologists can see their deepest secrets. I've seen a banker turn pale when I've asked him if I could ask him a few questions about banks and money, while dozens of people, in the course of a casual conversation, have nervously asked me, 'Are you psychoanalysing me?', that is, 'Are you seeing into the deepest recesses of my being?'

Some parents tell their children that God knows what they are thinking.

If God made us, He equipped us puny creatures with aggression to help us to survive in a hostile world, and with imagination to let us express our aggression towards one another in thoughts rather than in deeds.

When we are children, we become aggressive because parents necessarily frustrate us. Frustration leads to aggression. Children soon discover that they can vent their aggression in fantasy, allowing them to both murder (in fantasy) and preserve (in reality) their parents.

But if God can read your thoughts, and if anger and aggression are wicked, your own truth ceases to be your own certainty and becomes instead a source of shame, guilt and confusion.

It's no wonder that some people come to feel that their thoughts are known to powers outside themselves and that these powers insert thoughts into their minds.

Some parents know that it is important to recognize and respect their child's own truth. However, knowing your own truth and hanging on to it no matter what is not without its problems. My friends Galen and Helen have brought up their daughter Naomi to know her own truth. Naomi has always been allowed to say what she thinks. Now she is a beautiful sixteen-year-old. Recently Galen said to me, 'She's utterly fearless. I'm afraid for her.' People alienated from their own truth often envy those who aren't and will seek to do them harm.

Naomi said, 'Why should I be afraid of people? They're just people.'

Surviving as a person knowing your own truth is a matter of deciding in an imperfect world which imperfections are the easiest with which to live.

Some children manage to hang on to their own truth, or at least some part of it, because they are brought up by parents who are too lazy, or too busy, or too inconsistent to police the child's every act. These parents might, however, on occasion mock or punish their children when they reveal their own truths. Their children soon learn to keep their thoughts to themselves.

What effect this has depends on how well the children think of themselves.

If they manage to hang on to some self-confidence they become revolutionaries, inventors or artists who can decide which of the imperfections of this imperfect world they will accept and which they will try to change. The revolutionaries might not lead a revolution except in their own lives. They are critical of society and fail to conform. The inventors and artists preserve something of the child's fresh vision of the world and out of this vision develop other possibilities.

Children who grow up knowing that they see the world in their own individual ways but who don't think well of themselves feel that the fact that they see things differently means that there is something wrong with them. They think, 'I oughtn't to feel like this. I ought to be like other people.'

Some children are brought up by parents who police their every act and forbid the children to have their own truths. Such children cease to recognize what their own truth is.

Some of these children, as adults, know only what they *ought* to think and feel and not what they *do* think and feel.

Others sense their own truth as a void inside themselves. They say, 'I don't know what I feel,' and 'I don't know who I am.'

To be born deaf and blind to the world around us is an immense handicap to living a full life, but to become deaf and blind to yourself is a far greater handicap – it means losing most of the unique ability

we have as human beings to reflect upon our thoughts and actions and the world around us.

It means too losing the only reliable sense of certainty in an uncertain world, the certainty of knowing what you think and feel. If you have this you have a benchmark against which you can measure every event you encounter.

However, to know what you think and feel you need to be able to *accept* what you think and feel. This isn't always easy.

Parts of our own truth might cause us pain and fear, and so

we try to hide them from ourselves. A friend told me how her
parents had always seen her as the good daughter while her
sister was the bad daughter. She had accepted this role because
she thought that by being good she could stop her parents
fighting one another and punishing her sister for her supposed
wickedness. Now in her forties, she says, 'I'm just starting to
recognize the anger I felt because I had to be the one that kept
the family together.'

Parts of our own truth can cause us shame and guilt. If you've
been brought up to believe that anger is wicked and that you
have no right to be angry, no matter what is done to you, you
have to shut away in your dark cellar all your angry thoughts
and feelings. Then you can say to yourself, 'I never get
angry.'

This, of course, is a lie.

Telling yourself that you don't get angry, indeed that you
have no need for anger, is as realistic as telling yourself you
don't breathe and have no need to breathe.

Here is one of those relative truths for which I have yet to
encounter an exception:

**Provided you've got a good memory you can lie to other
people and get away with it, but you can never get away
with lying to yourself. Lying to yourself always leads
to disaster.**

People who deceive themselves deceive themselves about
deceiving themselves.

I've met many people who have led long lives of self-
deception. They do not enjoy close relationships, for how can
someone know *you* if you are always pretending to be someone
else? Some of these people have a history of failed relationships.
Others have managed to acquire a long-suffering spouse (usually
a wife) who believes that to be a good, acceptable person she
must protect her husband from the consequences of his folly.

*If you want to have a sense of security in an insecure world, and
to have good relationships with the people who matter to you, you
must know and accept your own truth.*

CHAPTER 4

You and What 'You' Is

'YOUR OWN TRUTH' might sound like some solid mass of gold at the centre of your being, but actually it is your whole being.

Your whole being is your evolving, changing structure of meaning which came into existence in the womb and ever since has been growing and changing. It is the sum total of all the conclusions you have drawn and are always drawing from your experience, all your ideas, attitudes, expectations, opinions and beliefs.

Whenever I try to describe our structure of meaning I often use a sentence like, 'You created your structure of meaning.'

This sentence has the same form as the sentence, 'You wrote a book.'

We all know that this second sentence is about two things, you and the book. But the first sentence isn't about two things. You and your structure of meaning are one and the same thing. To be accurate I should say, 'Your structure of meaning created your structure of meaning.'

There is no little person, no soul, spirit, self, person or identity inside you busily constructing your structure of meaning. Your structure of meaning is you, your soul, spirit, self, person, identity.

If a structure of meaning can survive the death of the body, when you die and go to heaven you/your structure of meaning will be busily making sense of heaven just as you/your structure of meaning is busy making sense of the world.

If you understand that you are your structure of meaning you

will know what is happening to you when you make a serious error of judgement.

To feel secure you/your structure of meaning has to feel that your structure is an accurate representation of reality. Then you can say to yourself, 'This is me, this is my life, the world is such and such and my future will be so and so.'

Perhaps as part of this secure structure of meaning you are saying to yourself,

'I have my career mapped out and it's all going to plan'

or

'My partner and I love one another and we'll be together for the rest of our lives'

or

'If I'm good nothing bad can happen to me.'

Then one day you discover that your judgement is wrong.

You lose your job, your partner leaves you, you are struck by some terrible disaster.

If something like this has happened to you, you'll know what it feels like when you discover that you've made a major error of judgement.

You feel yourself falling apart.

You feel yourself shattering, crumbling, even disappearing.

If you know that you are your structure of meaning, you'll know that what you are feeling is your structure of meaning falling apart, and necessarily so because it has to break apart in order to re-form into a structure which is a more accurate representation of reality. You have to re-plan your future, or build a life without your partner, or modify your religious or philosophical beliefs. This process is unpleasant and scary, but if you understand about your structure of meaning you'll be able to look after yourself while you go through it.

However, if you don't know that you are your structure of meaning you'll become terribly, terribly frightened.

If you don't understand that you are your structure of meaning you might resort to desperate defences to try to hold yourself together and to ward off the fear.

You might become too scared to go outside because you fear that if you do the terror will kill you, or that everyone who encounters you will reject you because you've done something completely unacceptable like vomiting or fainting.

You might get frantically busy, hoping that by being very active and pretending that everything is all right you can run away from the terror.

You might start tidying and cleaning everything, checking

and rechecking that everything is safe, all in the hope that if you get everything under control you'll be all right.

You might become convinced that certain things have special meanings and that you are the object of special attention from certain powers, all in the attempt to make an unpredictable world predictable.

You might decide that you alone are responsible for the disasters that have befallen you and that you are too wicked a person to be close to others and be part of the world.

If you don't understand that you are your structure of meaning when you feel yourself falling apart you think that you are going mad.

If you then resort to one of those desperate defences, other people who share your lack of understanding will also think that you are mad.

Psychiatrists will tell you that you have a mental illness. They'll say you're agoraphobic or manic or compulsive-obsessive or schizophrenic or depressed. If you become a psychiatric patient, over the years you'll be given all these diagnoses – and many more fancy ones besides.

Yet all that happened was that your meaning structure hadn't in some respects reflected reality accurately enough.

Whenever we discover that we have made a major error of judgement we question every other judgement we have made. Such doubt loosens the other parts of our structure of meaning and so it all feels like it is falling apart.

Even when we understand that this is what is happening, the shock of the discovery of our error is followed by pain, anxiety, disappointment, disillusionment and varying amounts of anger and resentment. (At the same time there can be a sense of exhilaration and freedom. The day after I discovered I had misjudged the degree of my husband's faithfulness I went into a state of shock AND I bought myself a complete new set of make-up. Part of me was saying, 'Whoopee!' because the freedom I longed for was now mine.)

Just as our body following illness or accident will strive to heal itself, so our meaning structure will strive to re-organize itself and align itself with reality in such a way that we can go on living with a sense of security and hope.

But, just as when ill or injured we have to assist our body to heal itself by taking care of ourselves, so when our meaning structure has to reform itself we have to assist it by recognizing that, 'By changing I'll survive,' or even, 'By changing I can improve my life.' We need to be prepared to let go of some cherished ideas and to modify others. Unfortunately our vanity often prevents us from doing this.

If your meaning structure still contains ideas like

'The only job I can have is one which commands a top salary'

or

'I can never be happy without my partner'

or

'The world has to be the way I want it to be'

your meaning structure is prevented from re-forming itself in such a way that you can feel at peace with yourself and find new ways of creating happiness and security.

Whether you want to change or not, a large part of your meaning structure is changing all the time. Every experience is a new experience, even if it is like a past experience. I'm sure you've met someone at work who's had one year's experience twenty times over, but even non-learners change. They just don't recognize that they've changed.

However, some parts of your meaning structure stay relatively stable over time.

For instance, the meanings you created when you were a baby so as to be able to tell whether an object was close to you or far away remain fairly stable, though as you get older you might need glasses to let you see the world as being crisp and clear.

Most of us form a meaning about what gender we are and stick with that throughout our lives, though a few people become increasingly convinced that their family have assigned to them an inappropriate gender and they do what they can to bring society's assessment of their gender into line with what they now experience.

Some of us hold for all of our lives a belief in, say, the existence of God or the natural supremacy of our nation, while others change their beliefs over time. A person might believe in God for the entirety of his life but his image of God might change from an old man on a cloud to an unknowable power.

Every part of our meaning structure is connected to every other part. The part we are conscious of at any one time is really quite small, but the unconscious parts, whether buried in our cellar or just a part we haven't had any cause to use for a long time, are linked to our conscious part and to one another.

Many people like to delude themselves that they can split their meaning structure into parts which have absolutely no connection with one another.

One extremely popular delusion, especially prevalent in the sciences and the professions, is that you can isolate your personal views and feelings and not allow them to play any part when you make an objective judgement. In psychoanalytic circles this is known as the defence of intellectualization.

Of course, when you are considering a subject which is far removed from your personal life it is possible to take a multitude of factors into consideration and weigh the evidence carefully. However, the more the subject affects you directly the less you can do this. In following the fortunes of the England Football Team I am quite dispassionate about who should be manager, but whenever I was driving from Huddersfield to my home in Sheffield late on a Saturday afternoon and there was an important match being played at Sheffield Wednesday's ground at Hillsborough my views about football and its fans would become distinctly emotional as I battled through the traffic. Nevertheless, even when a subject doesn't affect me personally, the only way I can make any sense of it is in terms of my past experience, that is, my meaning structure. I have nothing else on which to draw.

The delusion of objectivity allows many of those who regard themselves as the intelligentsia to believe that they are entitled by their education and intelligence to pontificate on all and sundry. Their education and intelligence have failed to make them aware that they cannot perceive reality directly, that all they have are the interpretations which they have acquired, as we all have, from their personal experience.

If people do not know this they cannot identify just which part of their structure of meaning is influencing their judgement. They then offer spurious reasons for the opinions they hold. They angrily reject any suggestion that there is a connection between their childhood experience and their current opinions or, as a member of that most privileged group, the White, Middle-class Male, they claim that they and they alone have the education and intelligence to know what is best for everyone else.

Such a way of thinking requires little mental effort. In contrast it took me some time and effort to work out that I held approving views about football because my dad approved of football, but, if a particular football match prevented me from doing what I wanted, which was to get home quickly, I wanted to banish football from the face of the earth.

One version of the delusion of objectivity is the belief that politics is totally separate from our personal lives. The feminists who created the slogan 'The political is the personal' were derided by their male critics for being weak-minded and emotional. Yet you can't even draw breath without being affected by politics. Even the quality of the air you breathe has been affected by the decisions made by politicians about pollution.

Psychologists have contributed to our lack of understanding of ourselves by the way they have traditionally separated individual psychology from social psychology, as if you as an individual are separate from the society in which you live. Yet you are a social animal and could not survive without being able to interact with other people.

Intellectualization isn't the only delusion about the supposed divisions in our meaning structure.

Where the next delusion is concerned we fall into two groups.

We have all been taught one basic delusion, namely that we can separate our experiences from our emotions. Having acquired this delusion, some of us believe that we can dispose of our emotions and just have our experiences. Psychoanalysts call this the defence of isolation and often call such people obsessive-compulsives or introverts. These are the people who can suffer a disaster but still say, 'I wasn't upset.'

Others of us believe that we can dispose of our experiences and just have our emotions. Psychoanalysts call this the defence of repression and often call such people hysterics or extroverts. These are the people who will say, 'Do people really remember their childhood? I don't,' and then 'I don't know why I get so upset.'

Of course there are often situations where it's a good idea to keep your emotions in check or to banish certain thoughts from your consciousness, but if you kid yourself that you have disposed of these inconvenient aspects of your structure of meaning once and for all you will soon be in trouble. If, at some later stage, you don't recognize and deal with these aspects they will come back to haunt you and disrupt your life.

You will have noticed that when a death occurs in a family some family members are very calm and sensible and able to attend the deathbed, agree to an autopsy and arrange the funeral, all without showing many signs of grief. Other family members become distraught with grief, so much so that they cannot contemplate, much less discharge, those difficult tasks which arise from the harsh reality of death.

If you are one of those people who in a crisis become very calm and sensible you need at some later time to allow those unacknowledged feelings of rage and fear to surface and express themselves without any sense of shame or guilt on your part. The people around you need to be able to accept your feelings without criticizing you or rushing to 'make it better'. If your loved ones lack such wisdom, you need to find a private place where your feelings can come in the full flood which brings its natural conclusion.

If you are one of those people who reacts to a crisis with great emotion and a refusal to acknowledge those aspects of the situation which terrify you most, you need at a later time to confront those aspects of the situation which you so wish to deny. These aspects are not simply part of the harsh reality of life but aspects which carry a personal threat to you: the threat of loss, of being abandoned, of being utterly alone. Such a confrontation is easiest done in the company of people who do not criticize you or rush to 'make it better', but developing the skill of quiet and solitary contemplation will stand you in great stead.

Emotions which have not been recognized and dealt with come back in unbidden rage or 'irrational' tears or in unpleasant dreams. They will interrupt the efficient functioning of the auto-immune system, thus making the way clear for the development of disease and disability.

A less popular delusion but one which has caught the imagination of the media is that of believing that you can divide your meaning structure into different people. Psychiatrists call this Multiple Personality Disorder. It is an extension of the second delusion where you bury your experiences and invent another role to play.

Women who, as children, have been repeatedly sexually assaulted often report how they tried to split themselves in two, in effect becoming two people, a sexual being and an ordinary girl. While enacting one role they tried to forget that the other role existed. Acquiring the skill necessary to use this desperate defence against annihilation can lead a person to create more and more separate 'selves'.

If a person does this without reflection upon what she is doing it is not difficult for her to claim that it all 'just happened'. The professionals and others who become involved with these multiple selves can be so caught up in the drama that they might never try to discover the gross cruelty the person suffered which made such a defence necessary or, equally foolishly, they might decide that sexual abuse is the one and only cause of the person's behaviour.

Whatever you might like to tell yourself, your meaning structure is all of one piece and each part is connected to every other part. Each part can influence every other part. It is the sum total of all the conclusions you have drawn and are always drawing from your experience, all your ideas, attitudes, expectations, opinions and beliefs. You and your meaning structure are one.

CHAPTER 5

You and How You Feel About Yourself

SOME PARTS of your meaning structure don't have much influence on the rest of your meaning structure. You mightn't be greatly concerned about what kind of biscuits you have for morning tea or whether your aunt sent you a Christmas card, although if pressed you would admit that you prefer a crisp biscuit to a gooey chocolate mess or that you do think it important that family members keep in touch.

However, there are two structures in your meaning structure which are central to it and influence every other part.

They are:

1. How you feel about yourself
2. What the top priority is in your life.

I have talked about how we are all born full of unselfconscious self-confidence and how we lose this. We become self-conscious and so acquire a vital part of our meaning structure, namely, 'How I feel about myself.'

Having a visual image of an idea, even if it bears no relation to reality, can help in understanding that idea. Suppose you imagined your meaning structure to be not you-shaped, coterminous with your skin, but egg-shaped. If you stood it on end and pushed a skewer from top to bottom the passage of the skewer through the egg would mark the central position of the particular meaning structure, 'How I feel about myself.' Every other part of your meaning structure is attached to and revolves around this structure.

Now let's think of this central meaning structure as being a straight line or dimension which measures just how you feel about yourself.

At the top is that blissful state of feeling at home with yourself, not criticizing yourself, feeling that you've got everything right and that everyone who matters to you loves you.

At the other end is that most unpleasant state of feeling yourself to be alien and hateful, criticizing yourself for everything you have ever done and ever been, feeling that you have made a mess of everything and that everyone who knows you hates and rejects you.

Daily, how you feel about yourself moves up and down this dimension.

Most days there mightn't be much movement.

If you've retained or recovered some of the self-acceptance with which you were born you stay above the mid-point, but if your cellar is jam-packed full of the darkness which you see as bad, you hover between the mid-point and the depths of self-rejection.

In both cases, there might sometimes be a wild swing to the heights when something has gone extraordinarily right for you, or to the depths when something has gone devastatingly wrong.

Whenever you have to make a decision on any matter, however trivial or important, and whenever you create an interpretation about any matter, how you feel about yourself will play an essential part in that process.

A simple example.

You wake up in the morning and you think, 'I feel sick.'

What are you going to do about this?

If your feeling about yourself is in the top half of the dimension your thinking will go along the lines of, 'I'll take care of myself,' 'I'll stay in bed,' 'I won't go to work today,' 'I'll get the doctor to come and see me.'

If your feeling about yourself is in the bottom half of the dimension your thinking will go along the lines of, 'I can't stay in bed. I've got work to do,' 'I've got to go to work or they'll think I'm slacking,' 'I can't trouble the doctor.'

While you're lying there making up your mind what to do you switch on the radio and listen to the news. There is the usual litany of tragedies, deaths, destruction and infamy. How you interpret all of this depends on where you are positioned on your 'How I feel about myself' dimension.

If your feeling about yourself is in the top half of the dimension you don't feel threatened personally by such events although you might deplore the stupidity, immorality and greed of the people who brought such events into being. You might even heighten your resolve to improve the world in some way.

If your feeling about yourself is in the bottom half of the dimension you do feel threatened personally by such events. You deplore the stupidity, immorality and greed of the persons who brought these events into being, but all this only supports more strongly your conclusion that the world is a wicked, evil place and that all the future holds for you is despair, doom and disaster.

The better you feel about yourself, the better the world and the future look.

The worse you feel about yourself, the worse the world and the future look.

If you don't understand how your decisions and your interpretations are influenced by how you feel about yourself, you will, like those people who suffer from the delusion of intellectualization, think that you are making decisions and interpretations on purely objective grounds when in fact you are not.

If you don't realize that how you feel about yourself is an interpretation and instead think that your feeling of badness and unacceptability is an irrefutable fact of the universe, a part of the natural law, you will always feel trapped and miserable, no matter what good fortune comes your way.

If you do realize that how you feel about yourself is an interpretation you know that when good fortune eludes you or friends betray you or you make mistakes you are free to create whatever interpretation suits you best. Be miserable if you want, or lay the blame on others, feel guilty and vow to improve,

i am thE oldest son of A titLED faMiLY
wiTh LAnd THaT rivaLs casTLE HOWaRd. My motHER
died young, as a cHild, I had 24 nannies— whenever I
grew attatched to one, my father repLaced hER.
I was pErmanENtly Cold And bulliEd At schooL.
IN holidAYs i slAUghtEred aNimALs brED foR the
purpose. i grew up To mArry A womAN to whom I No
LongER spEAK. i'vE HaD a LifE Of cOMPLETE privilEGe and
total EmoTional DeprivAtioN.

enjoy the comfort of self-pity, or tell yourself that things are
bound to get better.

You are free to choose.

Choosing to change how you feel about yourself and actually
changing can be very easy. It can also be very difficult for three
important reasons.

The first reason has to do with our relationships with other
people.

Suppose you're one of those nice, quiet, amenable people
who never disagrees with anyone and who always fits in with
what other people want. You do this because you think that
this is what being a good person means, but as a result other

people use you and trample over you. At work you get the jobs no one else wants and at home the family take you for granted. So you decide to change.

You make a very big change. You give up judging yourself on a 'good/bad' dimension and choose a 'making the most of my life' dimension. From now on all your decisions will be based on what you need to make your life satisfactory. You will still continue to be kind, caring and helpful when you feel it is appropriate but you will no longer be at everyone's beck and call. You state your needs and where necessary you criticize and argue. You now feel much happier.

Are your friends and family pleased with your change?

Not for a minute.

If you change they have to change. They have to see you differently. They have to behave differently towards you. They don't mind you being happy but not at their expense.

So they decide to push you right back where you were.

Just how they try to do this can range from violence ('She answered back so I hit her') through guilt ('I never thought I'd see the day when you wouldn't take care of your mother after all I've done for you') to humiliation ('You must be crazy'). Any attempt to do anything that you haven't done regularly before can be met with a hand applied to your forehead with the implication that you must be in delirium to behave in this way.

You have a choice – defend your own interests or be conquered.

The second reason why change can be difficult has to do with secondary gain. You might be suffering but you're also getting something out of it.

I used to run courses on self-confidence which were attended by business and professional men and women who felt that they were lacking in self-confidence. At the beginning of the course I would ask them to write down their answers to several questions, one of which was, 'What advantages do you get out of lacking self-confidence?' There would be protestations that there were no advantages but then everyone would settle down and list the advantages of not thinking much of yourself.

The most popular advantage was that you don't have to do anything where you might fail. You entered only the races where you knew you would win. Many women spoke of how, by being hesitant and uncompetitive, they ensured they were liked. One woman said she feared that if she became self-confident her husband would cease to pay her the wonderful compliments which he did when he was trying to persuade her to attend some important social function.

It is the fear of losing their advantages which stops most people from changing.

The third reason which stops people from changing has to do with the nature of change itself.

Our meaning structure is changing all the time as every moment we are encountering a new situation. However, most of the time we interpret the new situation as being just like an old one and so our meaning structure easily accommodates this new interpretation within the old ones. Certain of our ideas stay the same no matter what happens. As Jack Lyle, my psychology lecturer in Sydney, used to say, 'The older we get the more like ourselves we become.'

However, those ideas which form the 'How I feel about myself' dimension can undergo two kinds of change, first-order change and second-order change.

In first-order change we simply move up and down on the dimension. Today you can be right at the bottom of your 'good/bad' dimension because you're worried that the work you've done doesn't meet the necessary standards. Tomorrow important people praise you for your work and you go right up your 'good/bad' dimension.

Second-order change occurs when we abandon a dimension as being salient in how we judge ourselves and put another in its place. You might have measured your value along the dimension 'the best footballer in the world/the worst footballer in the world' but at thirty you decide that, contrary to what you had always thought, life does not end at thirty and that you will now measure yourself on the dimension 'the best football

AGE hAS given me a cerTain
kind of FReedom. wHen I WaS YOunGeR
I mindEd more whAT people said.
I AM beyond THaT NOW. I HAVE to satisfy
mY Own feelings abouT things. I simply
MUSt WAtCH "Neighbours" whatever elsE is
happENING IN MY LIFE!

manager in the world: the worst football manager in the world'.

Changing from a 'good/bad' dimension to some kind of 'making the most of my life' dimension is a second-order change. It is this change which is much more likely to ensure your happiness.

However, a second-order change means that every other part of your meaning structure will change. Every part of your meaning structure is connected directly to every other part and when the central dimension of how you feel about yourself changes, your whole meaning structure changes.

No wonder friends and family object!

There's great pleasure in being able to set your own agenda!

CHAPTER 6

You and Your Priorities

NOW TO the second part of your meaning structure which influences every other part of your meaning structure: what the top priority is in your life.

This is something about which I have been writing and teaching since the early eighties. I find that people respond strongly to what I say about this, but in doing so they fall into three groups:

1. Those who say, 'I've always known that about myself and others. I just didn't use the words that you use.'
2. Those who say, 'I've learnt something exciting about myself and other people. A lot of things have now fallen into place.'
3. Those who, no matter how often I explain, cannot see that I am talking about the reasons why we do something and not about a classification of people into two types. They say, 'I think I'm a bit of both.'

The people who fall into the third group are usually those who all their lives have directed their attention to the world around them and away from their internal reality of thoughts and feelings. They haven't developed to any great degree the skills of inspecting and assessing this internal reality and indeed they might feel that it is not right and perhaps somewhat frightening to do so.

Also in this group are people who have completely lost touch with their own truth. They know what they *ought* to think and feel but not what they *do* think and feel.

What this group of people is really saying is, 'I don't know what matters most to me.'

If you don't know what matters most to you, how can you make sure you get it?

What matters most to all living creatures, from the amoeba to *Homo sapiens*, is to keep on living. The purpose of life is to live.

I don't know how an amoeba or any other insect, fish or animal species experiences living, but I do know that for us *Homo sapiens* 'living' is far more than bodily survival.

We all do almost everything we can to survive physically as a body, but most of us would throw away our physical survival in order to survive as a person, that is, in order for our meaning structure to keep itself intact.

Many of us, when our meaning structure feels overwhelmed by demands, conflicts and anxiety, reach for some deadly nicotine, alcohol, cocaine or heroin.

Many of us, if our meaning structure did not want to be overwhelmed by shame and guilt, would fight and die for some cause.

Many of us, if our meaning structure did not want to be overwhelmed by loss and guilt, would relinquish our lives in order to preserve the life of someone we love.

Many of us, if our meaning structure interpreted its situation as, 'I cannot continue to exist in these circumstances,' would kill our bodies in the hope of preserving the integrity of our meaning structure. (More about suicide later.)

You might never have found yourself in a situation where you had to choose between surviving as a person (an intact meaning structure) or surviving as a body, but every moment of your life you are in the business of keeping your meaning structure intact (or rather your meaning structure is in the business of keeping itself/you intact). The way you've tried to organize your life, all the habits you've developed, all your pleasures and all your fears have developed as the means whereby your meaning structure tries to keep itself together.

Whenever you feel anxious it's because something has happened which your meaning structure sees as a threat to its integrity. Whether it's the passing anxiety of being late for a meeting or the drenching fear that awakens you in the darkness of the night, your meaning structure has seen a threat to its integrity. The threat is that of annihilation. You/your meaning structure will become nothing, a no-thing. You/your meaning structure will no longer exist and never will have existed.

Let's take this anxiety about being late for a meeting. With traffic being what it is today anyone can unintentionally be late for anything. Why is your meaning structure getting in a state?

It's not the lateness *per se* but what being late means to you. Your meaning structure knows exactly what being late means and doesn't need to spell it out to itself, but here I shall.

Suppose you said to me, 'I just can't stand being late for meetings.'

I would ask, 'Why is it important to you not to be late for meetings?'

Here I am asking you for *reasons*, why you do what you do. I'm asking you to tell me, not what other people think, or what we're all supposed to think, but what *you* think and feel. It's an exploration of your own truth.

Some people, about half of us, answer this question with something like, 'Punctuality is important to me. Being late is such a waste of time.'

I now ask, 'Why is it important to you not to waste time?'

'It's inefficient.'

'Why is it important to you to be efficient?'

'Because by being efficient I achieve what I want to achieve.'

When I ask, 'Why is it important to you to achieve?' it rapidly becomes clear that there is no further reason hiding behind this reason. This is your ultimate reason.

That sense of achievement is your ultimate reason. You mightn't be talking about fame and fortune. Even if you are, you're talking about these in terms of the sense of satisfaction of getting something done, of organizing and clarifying something and with that some sense of being a stronger, more competent person.

Thus for you being late means disorder, chaos, annihilation.

Now if this isn't ringing bells for you it's because if I had asked you, 'Why is it important to you to be punctual?' you would, like the other half of the human race, have answered differently.

You might still have talked about not wasting time and being efficient but when we got to your needing to achieve there would have been no sense of having gone as far as we could go. Instead there would be a further, more important reason.

Thus, when I ask you, 'Why is it important to you to achieve?' you start talking about other people, how, when you achieve people notice you, admire you, like you, even love you. When you don't achieve people ignore you, scorn you, dislike you, even hate you, and that means rejection, abandonment, annihilation.

By looking at the reasons which lie behind an apparently trivial decision like, 'I don't want to be late,' you can reach a reason, a meaning within your meaning structure, which lies behind every decision and every interpretation you make.

This part of your meaning structure which influences every other part is concerned with how you experience your sense of existence and how you see the threat of annihilation of your meaning structure.

This sense of existing as a person and the threat of being annihilated as a person we each experience in our own individual way. However, as I have just shown, this infinite number of ways falls into two groups which can be defined in very general terms.

1. Experiencing your sense of existence as developing, organizing, clarifying, achieving; seeing the threat of the annihilation of your existence as disorder, mess and chaos.
2. Experiencing your sense of existence as being in relationship to other people; seeing the threat of annihilation of your existence as rejection and abandonment.

Each of these definitions of two kinds of meaning structure runs to 25 words. A simple shorthand reference for each definition would be useful, but immediately there is the danger that this word would be seen as being one of the fictions in psychology which confuse and mislead. This is the notion that there are personality types.

Personality types are no more than ideas invented by psychologists in order to measure the characteristics of people in the way that zoologists measure the features of animals or geologists measure the composition of rocks. Personality types do not explain why individuals behave as they do.

Here I am not talking about personality types but two groups of individuals. When I say 'introvert' I mean a person who would fall into the first group, and when I say 'extravert' I mean a person who would fall into the second group.

One group is made up of those people whose ultimate reason lying behind their every decision has to do with developing, organizing, clarifying, achieving and with being frightened of disorder, mess and chaos. There is an infinite number of ways in which such people might interpret and express such meanings. Some might want to set the world to rights, while others want to devote their organizational skills to keeping their family in order.

The other group is made up of those people whose ultimate reason lying behind every decision has to do with creating and maintaining relationships and avoiding being rejected and abandoned. Some such people interpret and express these reasons by becoming successful entertainers and others by surrounding themselves with family and friends. Some, feeling too shy to attract lots of people, turn their pets or their possessions into people and maintain good relationships with them. This is one of the reasons why pets and fluffy toys are so popular.

What is it best to call these two groups of people?

At first I called them What Have I Achieved Today Persons and People Persons.

But these names ignored something very important. This is how we experience what we call reality. Let me explain.

While I'm writing this I'm hearing two voices. One is a voice from the radio beside me and one is the internal voice of my thoughts. Some of the things my internal voice says I am writing down.

Actually both these voices, the radio and my thoughts, are inside me. The radio voice is my meaning structure's interpretation of certain sound waves striking my eardrums and the internal voice is my meaning structure in action.

However, my meaning structure tells itself (me) which voice is outside me and which inside.

It's very important that my meaning structure gets this distinction right because if it doesn't (as can happen when 'How I feel about myself' plummets to the bottom and my meaning structure cannot make any reliable sense of what is going on) I won't be able to keep myself safe and other people will think that I'm mad.

Ideally your meaning structure should be able to distinguish what is going on solely inside you (your thoughts, feelings, images, memories) from what are interpretations of what is going on around you. Both sets of interpretations should seem real, so real that you can think of yourself as knowing two realities:

1. the internal reality of your thoughts, feelings, images, memories
2. the external reality of the world around you.

When you are sure that your interpretations are right, your interpretations feel *real*.

Let a little doubt in and your experience of your internal or external reality becomes less real. The reality takes on an 'as if' quality.

Some of us doubt our external reality more than our internal reality.

Some of us doubt our internal reality more than our external reality.

What Have I Achieved Today Persons doubt their external reality more than their internal reality. Under stress they find that external reality has become less real, even unreal, but their internal reality remains as real as ever.

I well remember this happening to me when I was seventeen and a very shy, frightened undergraduate at Sydney University. Returning from a visit home I got off the train at Central Station, expecting to be met by a friend who helped me a great deal in dealing with my anxieties about the university and the big city. But he wasn't there, and suddenly the whole of the station concourse became insubstantial and unreliable, a passing phantasmagoria of which I was an observer, not a participant. I dared not move. Then through the milling phantom figures came my friend, hurrying, smiling, pleased to see me. Central Station became real again, but I was white and winded by my experience.

People Persons doubt their internal reality more than their external reality. Under stress they find that internal reality has become less real, even unreal, but their external reality remains as real as ever.

In my experience at Central Station and all the other similar experiences I have had I have seen external reality grow unreal, but my internal reality of thoughts and feelings has never become unreal. I could not imagine what it would be like for my external reality to remain real while my internal reality became unreal. The first person who described this experience to me so that I could in some small way imagine it was my friend Peter. He said,

There was a time when I was staying with a great dear friend of mine, and when I went to the end of a long drive to catch a bus, and there was nowhere I had to go, nobody was expecting me anywhere. Therefore, if I didn't turn up anywhere, nobody would notice. I had just left some friends, I was estranged from my parents, and the marriage I had no longer existed, and I came to a sort of T-junction, a physical T-junction of a driveway and a road, but also in a sense a sort of, not an emotional T-junction, a life T-junction, and it didn't matter which way I went. Physically it wasn't important, it was neither here nor there, but from the point of view of how I felt, I felt sort of isolated and non-me. I felt as though I didn't exist, because my existence depended upon other people's recognition of me and my perception of me. . . . I saw it as a fact that I functioned in conjunction with other people and I had nobody to function with. Then I had great doubts about my own existence.[6]

Very sensibly we turn to and prefer the reality which seems the more real.

If your ultimate reason is concerned with the development and achievement of you as an individual you will consistently turn towards your internal reality.

What Have I Achieved Today Persons turn towards their internal reality. Hence the word 'introvert'. ('Vert' comes from the Latin word 'to turn'.)

If your ultimate reason is concerned with relationships with other people, you consistently turn towards your external reality because other people are in your external reality.

People Persons turn towards their external reality. Hence the word 'extravert'.

Unfortunately the words 'introvert' and 'extravert' are used most frequently to describe the way people behave. Someone who is shy, silent and unforthcoming is often described as being an introvert, while someone who is talkative and socially active is described as being extroverted (usually spelt with an 'o' rather than an 'a').

Here, however, the words are being used to describe people's behaviour and not to refer to the reasons why people behave as they do.

It is important to remember that

Two people can behave in exactly the same way but for very different reasons.

Thus two men might be devoted to their families and show the same kind of loving, caring behaviour.

If you asked each of them, 'Why are you devoted to your

family?' one might say, 'My family is my top priority. I love having them around me' while the other might say, 'It's important to me to be a good father. I want to achieve in life and I want to help my children to achieve.'

Or two women might be asked to speak at a conference and both refuse to do so.

However, if you asked each of them, 'Why did you refuse to speak at the conference?' one might say, 'I would speak if pressed but I can achieve my best by working behind the scenes, organizing the conference,' while the other might say, 'I wish I could get up and speak and impress an audience but I'm sure I'd make a mess of it and people would be disgusted with me.'

The second woman, who falls into the extravert group but is shy, might think of herself as being an introvert because she does not realize that behind all her decisions lies her number one priority of wanting people to like her and not reject her. She also might not realize that some of the people she took to be 'extroverted' actually had as their top priority a sense of achievement. In their teens or twenties they had realized that they lacked the social skills which extraverts can acquire easily very early in their lives and had set about learning these skills.

The differences between those people whose top priority is a sense of achievement and those whose top priority is relationships are considerable. (I have written two books about these differences, *Beyond Fear* and *The Successful Self*.) However, such differences can be obscured by the lack of discrimination in the language we speak and our unwillingness to tease out the subtle differences in our experiences.

One major difference is the amount of stimulation each group wants from the surrounding environment.

The group I call, for brevity's sake, people in the extravert group like lively surroundings and lots going on, while the group I call introverts prefer a high degree of peace and quiet.

My friend Linda, who had often heard me speak of the discomfort, even pain, that introverts like me feel when my immediate environment is too stimulating, felt that this must show that she too was in the introvert group. I thought she was in the extravert group, so we spent some time comparing our experiences.

Linda said, 'I can be with a crowd of people and just want to go away on my own. I start worrying whether I've said anything to upset them and whether they're tired of hearing me talk. I worry about what they're thinking about me.'

I could see that in such a situation she might want to leave before she was thrown out, but that wasn't what I experienced in a too stimulating environment.

In that situation I don't think about other people except, perhaps, to wish that they'd be quiet or not all demand my attention in one way or another. Rather I feel that everything is going out of my control and threatening to overwhelm me. Some time after I had left the situation I might worry about what I had said and done, but this would not be in terms of what other people thought of me but in terms of whether I had got things right.

The kind of worrying which Linda and I did, each in our own way, is part of the process of mastery, which is the process whereby we turn every experience into some kind of memory which fits into our existing meaning structure without requiring our meaning structure to make considerable changes.

Mastery deals with both the memory of the events and the feelings which these events arouse in you. Splitting your feelings from the memory and denying the memory (repression) or denying the feelings (isolation) is not mastery.

When a new experience is very much like many other past experiences our interpretation of it slips easily into our meaning structure. When your journey to work is uneventful, everything going to plan, mastering this experience takes no time at all.

But when you're delayed by an accident, or you rush out of the house without your wallet, you have to spend time thinking about the events and telling people about what happened until you have created a memory which slips into your meaning structure and no longer disturbs you.

People in the extravert group and people in the introvert group differ in how they do this.

Extraverts are good at forgetting inconvenient details. They are not concerned about making all the pieces fit because this is something which is important only for that part of their meaning structure concerned with their internal reality, which is less important to them than their external reality.

Whereas introverts, being always concerned with the state of their internal reality, want to get all the details to fit.

While extraverts are busy forgetting, introverts are rewriting the past.

Sometimes we have an experience the like of which we've never had before. Whether it is a joyous or unhappy experience, mastering it can take a long time. We have to talk about it, think about it, dream about it, even have nightmares about it before we can turn it into a memory with which we can live.

If the experience is a threat to our whole meaning structure and we don't understand that it is we can become very frightened. Psychiatrists call this Post-Traumatic Stress Disorder, but it isn't a disorder. It's our meaning structure discovering that the world is not what it had interpreted it to be.

Sometimes in such disasters our meaning structure discovers just how helpless we are.

In the terrible disaster at the Hillsborough football ground where in a dense crowd spectators were injured or crushed to death police and ambulance men and women on the other side of a high fence watched, unable to rescue the injured and dying.

Police and ambulance men and women are supposed to be helpful. Finding that in this situation they were helpless was a major threat to the meaning structure of each of them.

Some of them knew that there were limits to their helpfulness. They knew that when called upon they would do as much as they could to be helpful, but they did not blame themselves for not being able to do the impossible.

However, among those men and women were some who had built the notion of helpfulness into that core structure, 'How I feel about myself'.

Some were extraverts who had developed their sense of existence in terms of relating to other people by being helpful. They believed, 'If I am helpful other people will like me and not reject me.' Such extraverts abound in the helping professions, and in ordinary life they're the ones who 'can't do enough' for other people. Being made to feel helpless threatened their whole sense of who they were. They felt guilty because they had failed to be the good person they thought they should be.

Some were introverts who had developed their sense of existence in terms of being an efficient organizer who got things done. Any chaotic situation they would see as a problem and proceed to solve it. Being presented with a problem which they could not solve made them feel helpless, and that threatened their sense of who they were. They felt guilty because they had failed to be the good person they thought they should be.

Both groups were extremely upset by the same situation but for different reasons.

This event illustrates how our two core meaning structures are intermeshed.

How you feel about yourself affects how you experience your sense of existence and see the threat of annihilation, while how you experience your sense of existence and see the threat of annihilation affects how you feel about yourself.

If you're an introvert and your feeling about yourself is that you accept and value yourself (that is, your feeling about yourself is in the top half of the dimension 'How I feel about myself'), whatever life throws at you you meet with, 'It might take a while but I'll get this sorted out.'

However, if you're an introvert and your feeling about yourself is that you dislike and reject yourself (that is, your feeling about yourself is in the bottom half of the dimension 'How I feel about myself') every problem which arises, big or small, you meet with, 'I'm not going to be able to cope.'

If you're an extravert and your feeling about yourself is that you accept and value yourself whatever life throws at you, you meet with, 'Anyone who rejects me is a fool, and I'm not going to trouble myself with fools.'

However, if you're an extravert and your feeling about yourself is that you dislike and reject yourself, every problem which arises, big or small, you meet with, 'Everyone's going to hate me.'

It is tremendously important that you know what is your top priority, having a sense of individual achievement or having a good relationship with other people.

Of course we all want both. Life, however, often makes us choose.

Here is a dilemma which many people encounter.

Suppose you were faced with a situation where you could act only in one of two ways. If you acted in one way people would like you but you would not respect yourself. If you acted in the other way people would not like you but you would respect yourself. Which would you choose?

For introverts this is not a dilemma. Being liked is for them the icing on the cake, not the cake itself. They go straight for the second alternative.

For extraverts without a conscience this is not a dilemma. They go straight for the first alternative. They are not troubled by the need for self-respect.

But for extraverts who do have a conscience this situation presents a terrible dilemma. They want to do the right thing, but, oh, the fear of being disliked.

It is essential to know what is your top priority if you are to create a satisfactory life.

If you are an introvert you must make sure that there is something in your life which gives you a sense of achievement.

If you are an extravert you must make sure that your life contains at least one group of people of which you are a secure member.

Many unhappy, depressed wives and mothers are introvert women who have discovered that children and housework do not give a sense of achievement. Many of the apparently successful men who crash into disaster when they are promoted are extraverts who, having been very competent team men, cannot cope with the possibility of being the object of the dislike subordinates feel for those over them. Even when subordinates like their boss they reserve the right to criticize him.

Not only do we need to know what our top priority is but we need to remember that other people do not always share our priorities.

At a dinner party I told my fellow guests how my son had been at the Winter Olympics in Lillehammer where he saw the final of the men's ice hockey. It was, he said, 'a bunch of men on the ice trying to kill one another.'

My neighbour was horrified. Ice hockey was not only his passion but it was one of those marvels, a team game. He said, 'The greatest pleasure of all is to be a team member and for the whole team to move as one.' He went on at some lyrical length declaring it to be an Absolute Truth which all people would acknowledge – that there is no pleasure to compare with that of merging oneself with a team and for the team to take on its own identity and purpose. Bliss, utter bliss.

Across the table sat his wife. She must have heard such a paean hundreds of times. Her expression moved between boredom and disbelief. When she said, 'I don't understand what you're saying,' he repeated and elaborated what he had just said, but she simply shook her head.

And no wonder. Earlier, when she had been telling me about how she had begun her career as a social worker, she and I compared our experiences of working in some appalling hospitals for mentally handicapped people.

She said, 'I couldn't believe that hospitals could be run in that way. How could society let such places exist? Fortunately my senior social worker gave me some good advice. She said, "Don't think that you're going to change the whole system. Just pick out one or two areas and concentrate on those. That way you'll see something for your efforts."'

This is the best advice any introvert could be given. Try to organize the universe and you'll be defeated. Try to organize a small part of it and you've a chance of success.

Whatever your ultimate reason or your top priority is, remember that it is not a Universal Objective Truth which everyone shares.

It is your individual truth.

CHAPTER 7

You and Your Life Story

WHILE I'M writing this guide, every so often I stop to tell you a story. We all love stories – telling them and listening to them. The whole media industry exists because we love stories.

Actually stories have more importance than that of giving us pleasure. A story is the basic form we use to create meaning.

To understand what I mean by a basic form you might like to consider another basic form you know, that of a pot. Pots come in all sorts of shapes and sizes and have all sorts of uses, but whatever their shapes and uses they all have the basic form of a hollow shape with a base and an opening some distance above the base.

The function of the form of a pot is to hold things.

The function of the form of the story is to create meaning.

I'll explain this by telling you a story.

Suppose one morning when you're leaving for work you lock the doors and windows especially carefully because you know that the place is going to be empty all day. In the evening you arrive home and there, in the middle of the kitchen table, is a big brown paper parcel.

The presence of the parcel troubles you very much. You know that it is a parcel and not a bowl of fruit because in the past you've encountered parcels in many different stories. (If the object had been something you didn't recognize you would have been even more troubled.)

Even though you know the object is a parcel, you cannot give the parcel a meaning other than 'it is a parcel' until you can fit it into a story.

All stories have the same shape. There is a beginning, a middle and an end. Whenever we encounter just part of a story we feel dissatisfied, even troubled, until we can find the rest of the story. You have to discover the story about the parcel. You've got the middle of the story. The parcel is in your kitchen. How did it get there? What is in it? What is going to happen to it?

If all you know is the middle of the story, the parcel just doesn't make sense. But once you do establish the beginning and the end of the story the parcel does make sense.

Perhaps your neighbour, unbeknownst to you, had a key to your place and collected the parcel from the postman and in it you'll discover a nice woolly sweater knitted and sent by your mother. Or perhaps there is a Santa Claus and he came down your chimney to leave you a present . . .

We are born knowing about the form of a story.

If ever you've spent time in conversation with a tiny baby you'll know how the conversation starts with you and the baby exchanging nods and sounds and smiles. Together you can build these up into a little crescendo which reaches a crisis and then there's a falling away, a finishing, the denouement of the story. If the storytelling is interrupted before the denouement is complete the baby looks troubled, sometimes becoming distressed.

It is through the form of the story that we create and develop our sense of time passing.

Actually in your entire life all you ever experience is a continuous string of present moments.

All you ever experience is present time.

You are always engaged in constructing the present. Even when you are planning your future or remembering the past you are doing this in the present.

However, your meaning structure, using the form of the story, turns your interpretation of the present into constructions (memories) of the past.

Your meaning structure also creates the future.

Even though all we can ever experience is the present, we are born with the ability to anticipate the future.

While still in the womb, babies develop the ability to observe that one event always follows another and to use this observation to predict that the occurrence of the first will be followed by the second.

In the UK many babies are born believing that when they hear the theme music of the television soap *Neighbours* something nice will happen. This is because they are born to mothers who regularly switch on *Neighbours* just before they put their feet up and relax, thereby bringing to an end the bumpy ride the baby has when his mother is busy. Once born, the baby looks with pleasurable anticipation in the direction of the music when the programme is switched on.

Babies just a few weeks old will rapidly learn to shake the leg which is attached to a ribbon that, when pulled, will shake a cluster of small toys within the baby's vision. How wonderful to know that there is a future and that you are able to make that future happen!

The form of the story not only creates time, it also creates your sense of who you are.

Using the form of the story you create many stories, but the most important story you ever create is your life story. Your life story tells you who you are, what you were and what you will be.

When you were a little child you created the beginning of your story as you learned from the adults around you what sex you are, where you came in the family (oldest child or grandchild, youngest child or grandchild, and so on), your nationality, race, religion. Through family stories, photographs and videos you learn about a beginning to your story which existed before you were born.

In early childhood you began creating your own future as you learned what came next. 'Eat your vegetables and then you can have some ice cream.' 'Granny's coming tomorrow.' 'You'll be five next birthday and then you'll go to school.'

Your parents and teachers told you what your future would be, and at the same time you created your own future.

You thought about what sort of person you would become and what you would do. You tried out different ideas in different stories until you more or less settled on one story.

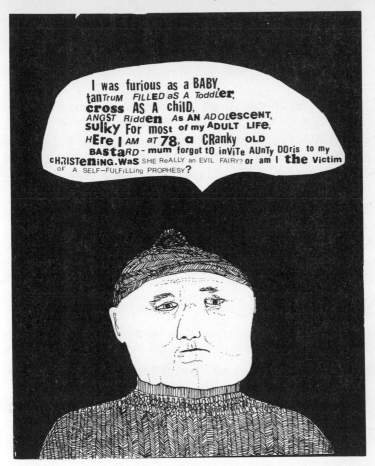

This would be your life story.

Whenever anyone asked you, 'Who are you?' or 'Where do you come from?' or 'What are you planning to do when you leave school?' you told that person something from your life story. Getting to know another person means the sharing of life stories.

These life stories are not fixed, eternal entities. Every time you think about your past life you do not pull out a memory in the way you can pull a file out of a drawer. Rather you construct a memory of an event, and every construction is a reconstruction with each reconstruction differing in some way from all the others. Similarly, every time you think about the future you construct an aim or wish or expectation, and such constructions change over time, just as the construction you call 'I' changes over time.

Your life story might have a basic theme which stays the same for many years, but just how this theme is elaborated in your story changes over time. Many little girls develop a life story based on the Cinderella story, but just how Cinders reveals her true worth and what attributes Prince Charming has will change as the little girls grow up.

Sadly, many little girls grow up believing that the Cinderella story must inevitably unfold in their lives just as night follows day. Prince Charming will arrive, fall in love with Cinders and together they will live happily ever after. The discovery of the dearth of Prince Charmings and their ability (or inability) to produce 'happily ever after' causes many women great disappointment and sorrow.

If you don't understand that your life story is something your meaning structure has constructed to give you a sense of identity and a sense of time, you might foolishly think that your life will be exactly as your life story predicts.

It then comes as a terrible shock when you discover, as John Lennon said, 'Life is what happens while you're making other plans.'[7]

But, if you have the wisdom to know that your life story is something you have simply created, when your life diverges from its story you know that you are free to create another story.

How boring your life would be if you always knew what was going to happen!

CHAPTER 8

You and Death

DEATH IS terrible, but it's not as bad as you think.

You mightn't want to think about death, but no matter what you do, death is very much part of your meaning structure.

First, consider the importance of contrasts in the way you create meaning.

The only way you can ever know anything is because you can perceive some kind of contrast or differential. Draw with a white pencil on a white sheet of paper. Unless the pencil line reflects the light differently from the paper, you won't be able to see it against the white background.

Newborn babies much prefer looking at pictures where the contrasts between the shades used are strong rather than at pictures where the contrasts are weak.

The only way you can know anything is to know its opposite. You know that there is light only because there is darkness and shadow. You know that there is perfection only because there is imperfection. You know that you are alive only because there is death.

Second, consider how you are always having to make choices.

If you lived for ever you could, over time, do everything you want to do – marry each of the people you fancy (provided they fancy you), try all the kinds of work that interest you, visit every place in the world as often as you want. All you would have to choose is in what order you would do these things.

But death exists and you have to choose. There is no time to do everything. Time and death set limits to what you can do.

When, as a small child, you were learning about time, you were also learning about death. Even in the most sheltered homes little children learn about death. Insects die, pets die, granny dies, people die on television.

You hear adults talking and you ask, 'What does "death" mean?'

No matter what fanciful explanations adults might give you, you soon discover that death can have only one of two meanings.

Death is either

the end of your identity

or

the doorway to another life.

Like every other meaning we create, each meaning for death has good implications and bad implications.

Some people like to say that they haven't made up their mind what to believe about death. This is a good way to make yourself miserable. Being unable to decide on a meaning for death means that while you have double the good implications you also have double the bad. You can worry about death being the end of you AND you can worry about Judgement Day.

The implications of the two meanings for death are very important because

whichever meaning you choose for death, that meaning determines what you see as the purpose of your life.

Even though you might try never to think about death and dying, you cannot help but think about what you see as your purpose in life.

You might never have made your purpose in life explicit to yourself, much less to other people, but you know when what you are doing does not fulfil your purpose in life. It is then that, even if you have no problems, you feel disgruntled, miserable, resentful, angry, guilty, frightened.

When you know that what you are doing does fulfil your purpose in life, even though other matters might be stopping you from feeling happy, you do have a sense of rightness and satisfaction.

How do the meanings which death can have determine your purpose in life?

Suppose you choose to see death as the end of your identity. Dying means that you-the-person disappears and you-the-body ceases to function and begins to decay. Not a nice prospect. How, then, can you manage to live with such a prospect?

By deciding to make your life as satisfactory as possible.

There are as many meanings for 'satisfactory' as there are people to hold them.

Introverts will choose meanings for 'satisfactory' that have to do with achieving something and avoiding wasting their life.

Extraverts will choose meanings for 'satisfactory' that have to do with warm, strong relationships and avoiding rejection and loneliness.

What kind of achievements and what kind of relationships are individual choices.

Suppose, instead, you choose to see death as a doorway to another life. Immediately you have to ask yourself, 'What kind of other life?' Of course it could be that the next life is considerably worse than this one, but only the most masochistic pessimist will choose such a meaning. Most people who believe that there is an afterlife worse than this life also believe there is an afterlife much better than this one. Every hell has its own heaven. This is to be expected, since for many people this present life is so terrible that they need to comfort themselves with the thought that in the next life they will be recompensed for their suffering.

So you decide that the next life is better than this one.

Immediately you are faced with the question of justice. Does everyone go to this better place? Do thieves, murderers and crooked politicians enjoy the same pleasures as those people who have never done anything wicked?

Obviously not. Certain standards must be met.

You might work out some very detailed standards for yourself or you might join a religion where the standards are very explicit. Entry into a better life after death could mean praying five times a day or never watching television.

On the other hand you might choose some general rules about honesty, tolerance, love and kindness, and judge each person's case, and your own, on its individual merits.

Whichever, choosing to see death as the doorway to another life means that you have to live this life in terms of the next.

Introverts define the standards of the next life in terms of achievement – somehow in every day and every way becoming a better and better person.

Extraverts define the standards of the next life in terms of establishing and maintaining good relationships, perhaps a special close relationship with God or sacrificing themselves in the service of others.

Each person, extravert or introvert, will create their own picture of the next life. Some people believe in an afterlife where this world still features, while others see an afterlife as being in some other space. There are as many heavens and hells as there are people to imagine them.

Belief in an afterlife, of whatever kind, is an attempt to deny that death exists.

All religions deny the existence of death. Christianity and Islam promise believers eternal life, Hinduism and Buddhism promise rebirth or merging with the Oneness of all existence.

Even though we discover death quite early in our lives, for quite some time after we both acknowledge and deny our own death. Sure, we've been told that everybody dies, but we say to ourselves, 'I'm the one exception. It won't happen to me.'

Then something happens which shows us that we are wrong. Usually it's a close brush with death such as James experienced when he was ten.

James had been in a car accident which he knew he had been very lucky to survive. A few days later, so his mother told me, he became quite distressed. For him death had become real. He

knew that one day, any day, he would die. While his mother was trying to comfort him he said, 'If I'd died, what would you have done with my things?'

She recognized that this was too important a question to be ignored or explained away. She said, 'I would keep some of your things to remember you by and some I'd give to your friends and some to Oxfam.'

James then told his mother precisely what she was to do if he died. He wanted to be cremated wearing his football strip. He listed which of his possessions she should keep for herself,

which his father and brother should have and which should go
to friends. The rest should be divided between Oxfam and Save
the Children.

Painful though it was for her, she carefully wrote down his
instructions. She knew that by organizing his funeral and leaving
a will James was giving himself a sense of having some control
over his death.

A sense of having control over their death is what introverts
want. What terrifies introverts most about their death is the
thought that they will lose the control they have over their lives
and that they will lose themselves in an unknown force over
which they can have no power. This for them is the ultimate
annihilation.

I think that dying must be very much like giving birth.

When I was pregnant I went to ante-natal classes and prac-
tised my exercises and breathing. I was sure I knew how to give
birth. I discovered that what I knew or didn't know made no
difference once the birth process took me over. I was not in
control, and the process did with me what it would as it ran its
course.

I expect the process of death will be much the same. An
introvert to the last, I hope I'm conscious when I die so I'll be
able to observe the process. For some of us introverts, even
when we can't do anything, observing and knowing gives us
the comforting illusion of control and order.

Extraverts are not terrified by the loss of control in death but
by the fact that death is the one journey which we each take on
our own.

When my dear friend Jill Tweedie, the loveliest of all
extraverts, was dying of motor neurone disease she talked to
me about what she was feeling as the disease ran its deadly
course. These were not dismal discussions. Conversations with
Jill always involved much laughter. When I told Jill how pleased
I was that her experiences supported what I say about why
extraverts fear dying, she told me she was glad to be able to give
satisfaction. We were both very pleased with ourselves when we
decided that the reason that Chinese emperors and Egyptian
pharaohs ordered that on their death hundreds of slaves and

servants should be killed and buried with them was because they were extraverts determined not to enter death on their own.

When her condition was diagnosed Jill was beginning to write the second volume of her memoirs. Ever since she was a teenager tapping out advertising copy Jill had enjoyed being alone with her typewriter. Now she told me that when she went into her study and sat at her desk 'the ferrets in my head start snapping at and biting me'. A wave of terror would rise up and engulf her. The ferrets that were busy telling Jill that death was real would also start their nasty work in the dark hours of the night when she could not sleep. They were quiet only when she was with her family and friends.

Jill did not hide her fear from us. She saw no reason to pretend a courage which she did not feel so as to make those with her feel more comfortable. Some of her friends, not wishing to acknowledge that they, like Jill, would some day die, pressed miracle cures upon her. Not wishing to hurt the giver, she accepted such gifts and even tried a few, but her clarity of vision, her life-long courageous search for truth prevented her from being lulled into a false hope with its aftermath of painful disappointment. She knew that the terrors of life cannot be defeated by flight or by self-delusion. She confronted her fears and so found ways of living with them.

Having a genius for friendship, Jill never lacked company, and we all wanted more of her time than she had strength to give. If love can go with us on the journey into death, Jill certainly did not make the journey on her own.

Here is the strangest thing about death.

Death plays such an important part in our lives, yet no one knows what death is.

While we are alive all we can ever know about death is that a person becomes strangely still and silent. We can know about the events which led to this stillness and silence, but while we are alive we cannot know what happens when this stillness and silence comes upon a person.

The strangest thing about death is that we cannot know what death actually is. Everything we think we know about death itself is a fantasy.

Your fantasy about death, whatever it is, always features you in the starring role, or at least there as an observer.

Your meaning structure, while always fearing its annihilation, cannot imagine its non-existence.

Even if you say, 'I see death as the end of my existence,' any picture which comes into your mind contains you there as an observer watching your death. If you say, 'Death is a blackness,' you see the blackness.

This is why most people have very strong feelings about whether they want to be buried or cremated. When asked why, they might talk about the impossibility of keeping a grave neat or not being a bother to relatives, and, even if they believe that death will end their identity, they, if obsessional introverts, see themselves being there deploring an untidy grave or, if self-deprecating extraverts, feeling guilty about being a bother. Often the reason for people's strong feelings about funerals has to do with what they see as the worst fate: waking up alive in your coffin and finding yourself either about to buried or burnt.

Your meaning structure cannot imagine its own non-existence. All you know about the experience of death is a fantasy.

This is why committing suicide is so foolish.

Your meaning structure knows you as being made up of you-the-body and you-the-person. If every part of you, you-the-body and you-the-person, wants to die, you don't have to kill yourself. You just give up and die. This is how many old people, many widows and widowers die. If every bit of you, you-the-body and you-the person, is convinced that your life is over, then you will die quietly and inevitably.

If you have to harm yourself in order to die, you do not entirely want to die. What you want is a painless way of being yourself without having to battle against a world which hurts and ignores you.

Death does not give you that. All that death gives you is death.

The reasons you give to yourself as to why you should kill

yourself are your interpretations of the situation and not, as you think, fixed, immutable Absolute Truths of the universe. You create a story about your death and its aftermath. You tell yourself you'll be at peace, or that your family will be happy, or that those who have hurt you will suffer unendurable guilt and remorse. But these are all stories, and real life, which you can neither predict nor control, will be different from your stories.

I have often heard people say that they want to die because death will end their pain. The cessation of pain can be a joyous experience. For the past few years every so often a small part of my alimentary system decides to go into a spasm. The pain is fierce, piercing and unrelenting and I can find nothing to relieve it. However, I eventually worked out that the spasm would last no more than twenty minutes so I simply wait as best I can for it to end. As the pain eases and vanishes a visceral feeling of joy suffuses me, so sweet a feeling that I used to think it was almost worth having the spasm in order to feel the joy. I have discarded that notion, but I do wonder whether the people who say that they long for the peace that death will bring are thinking that they will experience such joy. Yet if death is the end of their identity, they won't be there to know the joy.

In fantasies that your family will be happy when you die or that those who have harmed you will suffer remorse you assume that people will behave in the way that you want. What if you looked down from heaven and saw your loving family suffering grief or your enemies celebrating your passing! This is assuming that in the next life you can still see what is happening in this life. If this is so, your next life is unlikely to be happy because you will still be aware of the causes of your unhappiness and you will be impotent to change them. On the other hand, if in your next life you lose all memory of your present life, you won't know when you're happy because you won't remember what it is to be sad.

The notion of the next life creates more problems than it solves. There are more than enough problems in this life to trouble us.

Sometimes when life is particularly hard it is comforting to think that it doesn't go on for ever. Nevertheless, since death is inevitable, it is foolish to waste what life you have by bringing it to an early end.

Equally it is foolish to spoil your life by being terrified of death.

Think constantly and fearfully about death and you will be miserable.

Run away from death or deny death and you will be miserable.

Think carefully about the meanings you can give to death and you can find a meaning which will enable you to face death with courage.

The courage to face death gives you the courage to face life.

CHAPTER 9

You and Depression

NO ONE escapes depression. A great many people get
depressed, however briefly, at some time in their lives. You
mightn't ever get depressed, but some of the people close to
you will.

The experience of depression can be the very worst experience
you can ever have.

It can also be the getting of wisdom.

Nowadays people often use the words 'depressed' and
depression' when what they are talking about is not depression
but unhappiness or disappointment or anger or guilt or just
feeling a bit low. Psychiatrists often confuse unhappiness with
depression.

If ever you've been depressed you'll know that depression is
very different from unhappiness.

When you're unhappy, no matter what terrible disaster has
befallen you and even if nothing can be done to make things
right, you can be comforted by other people. Their love and
sympathy can sustain and warm you.

When you're depressed you can observe the people around
you being sympathetic and loving, but somehow their sympathy
and love cannot get through the barrier which surrounds you.
No matter what other people do, you are not comforted.

When you're unhappy, even if no one else will comfort you,
you'll comfort yourself. You'll look after yourself and talk to
yourself in a kindly way.

When you're depressed, not only will you not comfort yourself but you will even make things worse for yourself. You

criticize and hate yourself. You have become your own worst enemy.

When you are depressed you know that nothing in your surroundings has changed, yet for you the colour has drained out of the world and a barrier as impenetrable as it is invisible cuts you off from the rest of the world.

The experience of depression is the sense of being alone in a prison.

Someone who is depressed doesn't say, 'I feel as if I'm in a prison' but 'I *am* in a prison.'

If you want to find out if someone is depressed, ask that person, 'If you could paint a picture of what you're feeling what sort of picture would you paint?'

Each person will give a different image. Here are some images that have been described to me.

I'm in swirling water and being slowly sucked down.
I'm walking endlessly in the dark.
A drooping, dying flower wrapped in a blanket.
A child in a dark corner facing a wall.
I'm walking along an empty road that's going nowhere.
I'm on a quay and the last boat is sailing away. I can't leave the quay.
I'm in a box without doors or windows.
I'm in the centre of an empty, treeless plain. The plain goes on forever and I cannot move.

All these images have the same meaning. The person is alone in a prison.

If you asked the same question of someone who is unhappy the answer given would describe a miserable scene but there would be no sense of being trapped and alone.

It is this sense of isolation which makes depression so terrible. As all prison warders and torturers know, complete isolation for an indefinite period will break the strongest person.

Because the experience of depression is so exceedingly painful many people call it an illness and try to get rid of it. Yet, if ever you've tried to help someone who's depressed you'll know how the depressed person, while asking for help, manages to turn aside all your efforts.

You find yourself thinking, 'I can't get through to him' (you've come up against the prison wall which encloses him) and 'Why doesn't he pull himself together?' (This is not just an empty cliché. In some way you know that he is falling apart.)

What is happening is that you are trying to take that person's depression away from him but he is hanging on to it just like a person alone and drowning in a raging ocean will hang on to a life belt.

And indeed he is in something worse than in a raging ocean. He – his meaning structure – is falling apart and only the defence of his depression is holding him together.

Depression is not an illness.

Depression is a desperate defence which we can use to hold ourselves (our meaning structure) together when we feel ourselves falling apart and in danger of being annihilated. It's a defence we all can use – provided we have learnt how to be good.

Only good people get depressed.

What do I mean by 'good'?

When you measure yourself on your central meaning structure dimension 'How I feel about myself' you can, in theory, define this dimension in many different ways.

You might measure yourself on the dimension

The greatest footballer in the world . . . The worst footballer in the world

or

The most attractive woman in the world . . . the least attractive woman in the world.

Thus, with such a simple scheme, when you kick the winning goal or get paid a great compliment about your appearance you put yourself near the top of your 'How I feel about myself' dimension, and when you miss the winning goal or look in the mirror and think, 'I look ghastly,' you put yourself near the bottom of the dimension.

Most of us learn to use a more complex scheme in judging

I WAS broughT UP to be SO GOOD
THAT IF I EVEN thought OF DOING
SOMETHING WRONG I'D SMACK
myself.

Prisoner
of
conscience

ourselves. We think in terms of clean/dirty, kind/cruel, selfish/
unselfish, envious/not envious, unaggressive/aggressive, helpful/
unhelpful, honest/dishonest, loyal/disloyal, hard-working/lazy –
a whole collection of virtues and vices which I shall put together
under the heading good/bad. Most of us learn to judge ourselves
in terms of good/bad.

We try to do good and be good.

Even people whom you and I would think of as being
undoubtedly bad can use this measure. Peter Sutcliffe, the York-
shire Ripper, thought that he was doing good because he was
ridding the world of prostitutes. Hitler thought he was doing
good by ridding Germany of the Jews, while those Serbs who

support 'ethnic cleansing' see the process as making Serbia a better place. Isn't cleansing always good?

Because the only way we know something is to know its opposite, all these judgements are made up of pairs of opposites. To know 'good' you have to know 'bad', and to know 'bad' you have to know 'good'.

If you use good/bad to judge where you are on your 'How do I feel about myself' dimension, you have to keep thinking about how bad you are in order to decide how good you are.

If this is how you judge yourself, you are, in my terms, a good person.

A good person is someone who tries to be good while trying not to be bad. Just like the children in Michael Leunig's cartoon (see overleaf).[8]

Here Michael Leunig has set out brilliantly and succinctly what you must do if you want to get depressed.

This is the recipe for depression:

1. *Believe that you, your life and the world are exactly and unchangeably as you see them.*
2. *Believe that you are, in essence, bad and have to work hard to be good.*
3. *Believe that you live in a Just World where goodness is rewarded and badness punished.*
4. *Wait for a disaster to occur to you.*

The Father Christmas myth is one of the many myths which tell us that the world we live in is a Just World. Many people, as they get older, give up believing in Father Christmas but they don't give up believing in a Just World.

All religions teach that we live in a Just World.

Religions differ in what they call goodness and badness, rewards and punishments, but they all describe a Just World. If you're good you go to Heaven, or Paradise, or are reborn as a wealthy man, or leave the painful cycle of life and death to merge into Nirvana. The rewards and punishments mightn't be given to you in your life on earth, but the promise of rewards and punishments strongly influences your life on earth.

At this time every year, Santa Claus checks his records to see which boys and girls have been well behaved;

To see which children have not been too difficult for Mother and Father;

To see who has not been too selfish or demanding or disobedient;

To see who has been well brought up and is well mannered and pleasant and agreeable and cheerful and helpful and clever and good.

To these children he will give a gift which could become extremely useful to them in later life:

A big, thick book titled "UNDERSTANDING YOUR DEPRESSION"

Leunig

Many people who would say that they are not at all religious still believe that there is some over-arching Grand Design which ensures that somehow, in the end, wicked people get their just deserts while the good are compensated for their suffering. Such people are wont to say, 'If I didn't believe that in the end it all works out I would find my life quite meaningless.'

What they are saying is that if there is no Just World they will be robbed of the rewards to which they are entitled as recompense for their suffering and sacrifice in childhood. They have built their life story on this, and if there is no Just World their story can never come true.

When we are children we suffer a great deal in learning to be good. We sacrifice much of what we might have been in becoming the kind of person our family and society will permit us to be.

The only way we can accept our suffering and sacrifice is to be able to assure ourselves that it is not in vain. In the future we shall get our rewards. And so we create our life story, each of us in our own individual way but all with the same theme: 'I have suffered to be good but in the future I shall be rewarded.'

The fairy stories we are told as children reinforce the theme of our own story. Good little girls are rescued and loved for ever by Prince Charming and good little boys acquire power, wealth, the love of women and the admiration of all men.

The belief in a Just World gives a great sense of security. You feel you can predict what is going to happen to you. You feel that, by being good, you can keep yourself and your loved ones safe.

However, like everything else, the belief in the Just World has disadvantages as well as advantages.

Let me explain.

Whenever a disaster occurs we can ask two questions

How did this happen?

Why did this happen?

Answering the first question is the business of scientists, coroners and government inquiries.

We can all try to answer the second question because it is asking, 'Why, in the whole scheme of things, did this happen?' There are only three possible answers to this question.

1. *It was someone else's fault.*
2. *It was my fault.*
3. *It happened by chance.*

If the whole scheme of things is the Grand Design of the Just World then nothing can happen by chance. Disasters are always a punishment for wrongdoing. Believers in the Just World can explain why a disaster occurred only in terms of

1. *It was someone else's fault.*
2. *It was my fault.*

Believers in the Just World can explain the disasters that befall other people by saying that the disaster is a punishment for their wickedness. 'If she hadn't been dressed like that she wouldn't have been raped.' 'God has sent them a sign that they must change their ways.'

Blaming the victim has the advantage of saving the believer in the Just World from the pain of pity.

But what do you do when the disaster occurs to you?

Imagine:

There you are going along, you/your meaning structure assured in the knowledge that, even though you know how dangerous and unpleasant the world can be, you are safe because you have always done your best to be good. You mightn't be having a great time now but your life story tells you that your rewards will come.

Then one day something happens.

It might be some sudden, terrible disaster which strikes you or someone close to you.

Or it might be something which other people think is quite small but which shows you that you cannot go on kidding yourself that your life is turning out the way your life story predicted. Your life is actually very different from what you wanted it to be.

Whichever,

You/your meaning structure realizes that reality is not what you/your meaning structure thought it was.

You have made a huge error of judgement.

You feel yourself falling apart.

You are engulfed by terror.

Desperately you cast around for some explanation which will put you back together again. You ask, 'Why has this happened to me?'

You have at hand two answers.

Is it someone else's fault?

Is it your own fault?

You try putting yourself back together again by blaming other people. It's the fault of your parents, your partner, your friends, your boss, the doctors, the politicians, even God.

You get very angry and resentful.

Then you remember how wicked it is to be angry and resentful. How can you blame your parents! Doesn't the Fifth Commandment promise death to those who fail to honour their parents?

You can't blame other people. You can only blame yourself. You're an expert in blaming yourself. Good people always blame themselves and you're an expert in being good.

Now everything falls into place.

Now you're back together again.

The reason this disaster occurred is because you are an even more wicked person than you thought you were and this disaster is your just punishment.

However, this explanation has implications and immediately they come into operation.

You've always been somewhat reserved with other people in case they discover that nasty dark cellar at your centre. Now you must cut yourself off from other people completely lest they discover just how wicked and vile you are and they turn against you. Worse, the evil inside you could come in contact with other people and harm them.

You've always seen your past life as littered with evidence of how unsatisfactory you really are. Now your entire past is evidence of your wickedness. It is so painful to contemplate that you cut yourself off from it.

You've never seen your future as the fulfilment of perfect happiness because you did not think you deserved such a great reward. Now your future offers you nothing but punishment. You cut yourself off from it because you are terrified to enter there.

You've never really felt at home in the world. You've always felt unsure about yourself and your rights. Now you know that you don't have the right to be here, part of the world and everything that exists. Your wickedness excludes you.

Now you are alone, cut off from other people, from your past, your future and the world around you.

You are alone in the prison of depression, and as the days pass the torture grows worse.

What can you do?

You have a choice.

You can insist that the world *is* as you see it and that you *are* as you are. You can go on and on trying to make the world be what you insist it is. You can be like Lena's colleague:

He is a little over forty and totally self-destructive. He has terrible aggression towards 'all women'. My mental picture of him is a man lying under a thick cheese dish cover, hitting himself very hard on the head. And when someone tries to knock on the glass to reach him, he just looks up and shouts triumphantly (and accusingly): 'Just look how hard I keep hitting myself!' Sue, my other colleague, has been trying very hard to help him but his defence is intact. He writes terrible, aggressive letters, full of hatred, where he tries hard to prove how unattractive, worthless and unsocial he is and how it can never be otherwise. And everything that those who are trying to help him say or do is totally wrong. His mother and all women are cruel, attractive and without feelings. He is fighting hard to achieve exactly what he fears the most: that Sue will no longer have the strength to be his friend, and he will have lost her too, thus getting the confirmation that all women are cruel and without feelings and understanding.

or

You can discover that you, your life story and the world you see are not fixities of the universe but meanings which you have constructed and, since you constructed them, you can change them.

Then you can discover what Eileen discovered.

I'm twenty-nine now, and I look back at my twenties as being an extremely painful time. So much depression crammed into such a short period!

But, in a way I also look at that time as extremely fruitful. The most challenging, and stretching time of my life so far.

At the moment I feel very liberated. I was brought up with a rigid Catholic dogma. Part of my depression was coming to terms with the painful fact that there is no Universal Truth and it was up to me to accept responsibility for my life.

At the time I found that almost too distressing to contemplate, but now it is enormously liberating.

Now I know that I am the only one who can make the decisions. I am the one who can determine my destiny and happiness. I am no longer bound by some Universal Rulebook.

I lost my faith in a Catholic God as I perceived him, but the strange thing is I haven't lost my spirituality, that powerful feeling within which still recognizes and still feels a sense of good and hope despite all the odds.

Nowadays I'm good because it *feels* better, not because I think I'm going to get a reward in heaven.

Which solution do you prefer?
You are free to choose.

CHAPTER 10

You and Other People

DO YOU LIKE to believe that life can be understood in very simple terms? Do you feel that the pattern of life is actually straightforward, logical and rational, and that everything, properly understood, is quite clear-cut, either black or white, and that anyone who doesn't know this isn't being sensible?

If this is what you think then your relationships with people must cause you problems, or alternatively other people have problems with you.

Life, particularly that part of life which involves relationships between people, isn't at all simple, clear-cut, black or white.

This is because all our relationships involve a paradox.

A PARADOX OF LIFE

As an individual you cannot leave your meaning structure and enter that of another person; yet to survive as a person you have to have relationships with other people. Thus, every moment of your life you have somehow to be an individual and a member of a group.

How do we all manage this?
Answer: With difficulty.

Our need for other people is built into that basic dimension of our meaning structure, how we experience our sense of existence.

If you're an extravert you need other people because other people keep you existing as a person.

If, as an extravert, you have put yourself high on your 'How I feel about myself' dimension, you've probably discovered that you can be on your own for quite long periods of time. However, you do like to be sure that when you've finished what you're doing on your own there'll be some people waiting for you to join them. The thought of being utterly alone for ever is still terrifying.

If, as an extravert, you've put yourself low on your 'How I feel about myself' dimension, you're always frightened that other people will reject you. You try very hard not to be rejected. You work very hard at being kind, co-operative and helpful. You daren't get angry with anyone or speak your mind because you're sure other people will reject you if you do.

You might be so frightened of other people that you might spend a lot of time alone – but in the company of pets, or books, or furry toys, or pictures, or records of pop stars or pictures of sporting heroes. The objects and animals you have invested with the qualities of a perfect human being, while the pop stars or sporting heroes are fantasy figures who never reject you.

The good thing about turning animals and objects into people and having fantasy figures as constant companions is that you can turn them into the kind of person you want, someone who is eternally loving and loyal. You're loving and loyal to them in return.

If you're an introvert you need other people because other people keep you in touch with external reality.

Madness is often defined as being out of touch with reality. In this definition reality is what goes on around you. As an introvert you will know how easily external reality can become strange and unreal. You also know how real and secure your internal reality is (even when you're worried or upset) and how easy it is to dwell there.

However, if you spent all your time in your internal reality you'd soon lose track of what was happening around you. You'd start to make mistakes and say things which other people think are odd. Soon other people would be describing you as being eccentric, even mad.

As an introvert you need something in your external reality that keeps you paying attention to external reality. The other people who inhabit your external reality can make an effective claim on your attention and thus keep you sane.

But only if you've put yourself high on your 'How I feel about myself' dimension. Then you can treat your external reality as if it's real and have confidence in your guesses.

If, as an introvert, you put yourself low on your 'How I feel about myself' dimension, you don't have confidence in your guesses about external reality and other people can undermine your confidence even more.

When I was a child and made some observation to my mother about some happening which she didn't want to acknowledge, she would tell me I was mistaken or even lying. This so undermined my confidence in my judgements about external reality, especially about people, that I became very frightened about doing anything in relation to other people. Even saying hello became a torment because I couldn't be sure that I'd met the person before or, if I had, I'd remembered his name correctly.

I know that most of us have problems remembering names, but even though now I don't doubt the reality of other people, unless a person becomes one of the figures in my internal reality where the name is an integral part of that figure, I always feel that whatever name comes to mind whenever I meet an acquaintance cannot possibly be correct. I have a good memory for what people tell me about themselves, as the stories in my books attest, but where their names are concerned my mother's legacy is still with me.

There's no getting away from it, we all need other people for one reason or another.

It's no good trying to solve the paradox between the isolation of your meaning structure and your need of other people by deciding to be only an individual or only a member of a group.

A completely isolated individual goes crazy.

A complete 'groupie' takes on aspects of the meaning structures of the other members of the group and loses all contact with his own truth, thus becoming a victim of the whims of other people.

So, every day, we have to find a balance between being an individual and being a member of a group.

Isn't it curious that, even though we all need one another, we're so incompetent in getting along with one another? People seem to get together in order to misunderstand one another. Even people who, it would seem, would want to understand one another, such as lovers or parents and children, misunderstand one another.

Why?

Because they don't understand that we each interpret everything in our own individual way.

Because we don't understand that we each interpret everything in our own individual way, our relationships always have difficulties and often fail.

Of course, trying to understand another person's meaning structure is really hard work, requiring lots of careful listening and detailed thinking. Rather than work so hard most people prefer to think that anyone one who does not see things their way is either mad or bad.

It's very disturbing to discover that not only does another person see something very differently from you but that this different interpretation has as much claim to the truth as yours has.

Lena, who calls herself 'an introvert who has found out that people are important', found that understanding the differing interpretations made by introverts and extraverts helped her understand her colleague. She wrote:

I feel this difference especially in regard to a very extravert colleague of mine. We have been working in the same room of a research institute since 1989 and I really like her. She is a very warm, charming person with a profound interest in people and a wonderful sense of humour. Our families have met too. But her social life always makes me exhausted just to hear about: they are always having guests or being guests, big dinners and dancing – the

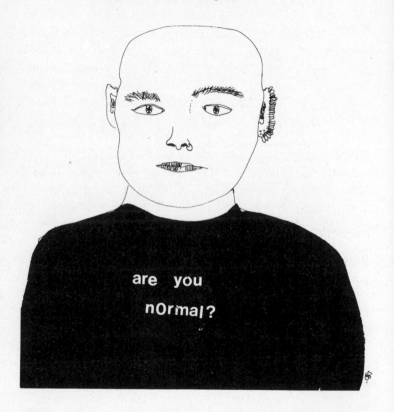

iT never worries ME IF people tHink I'm WEiRD bECause of the way I LOOK.

The strangest pERSOn I KNOW Lives in Ealing, wears A suit TO WORK, HAS 2·5 childrEN and A goldEN haired wife. he's my dad.

are you nOrmal?

works. (I sense, too, that she is worried about me not being social enough.)

The problem: Especially in periods when I have much to do (which is most of the time), I can feel a growing irritation towards her, and I can feel her feeling it, and suffering from it, and so forth. I knew why I was irritated: I got no help from her, and I could not understand why.

And then, in the evening I realized: We do not have the same basic concept of work. To her, work is yet another place to create and nurse relationships. After the last conflict she had with our boss she told me he keeps criticizing her personally (actually, the issue was that she is late every morning), but she claims she has no difficulty working for him – as she described it: 'He gives me work, and I do it and give it back.' That is work for her.

Whereas I have a very important relationship to my work. I do my job the very best I can, then I try to think out smarter ways of doing it, learning more, and making alterations, 'leaving my track'. And in the process I have lots of contacts with people inside and outside the institute. And enjoy every minute of it!

(How many couples take the time to work out, as Lena did, their differing perceptions of all the aspects of the life they share? Remember, opposites attract, and this applies as much to our meaning structures as it does to sex. I've often met couples who have told me that they were two introverts or two extraverts, but once we've got talking the basic differences in attitudes between an introvert and an extravert soon become apparent. The couples who thought they were two introverts were actually an introvert and a shy extravert, and the couples who thought they were two extraverts were actually an extravert and a socially skilled introvert.)

Often our language fails to capture the differences in our interpretations. For instance, both introvert and extraverts will say that they dread being utterly alone, yet if you ask them to describe what image they have of such aloneness, extraverts will describe themselves as fading away, vanishing and introverts will describe themselves as being alone on an empty planet.

How you interpret other people and how you create, maintain or destroy relationships depend on the two main dimensions of your meaning structure: how you experience your sense of existence and how you feel about yourself.

You interpret other people as you interpret everything else, that is, in the terms of your meaning structure.

Thus you interpret how you feel about another person in terms of how you feel about yourself.

The higher you place yourself on your 'How I feel about myself' dimension the more you like other people and feel at ease with them.

The lower you place yourself on your 'How I feel about myself' dimension the more you dislike other people and feel frightened of them.

The more you like other people the easier your relationships will be with them, and the more you dislike other people the more difficult your relationships will be with them.

On the whole, other people will take you at your own evaluation. If you value and accept yourself, other people will value and accept you. If you don't value and accept yourself, other people won't value and accept you.

Of course, many of the people who consistently put themselves low on their 'How I feel about myself' dimension are so unaggressive, unassuming, kind, and good to an astonishing degree that most other people like them very much.

However, if you've spent most of your life thinking that you are bad and unacceptable you can't have people liking you and thus upsetting your whole meaning structure. You hold firm to your view that, 'Whenever anyone says that they like me I know that that person is either a fool for not realizing how bad I am or a liar who knows how bad I am and is pretending to like me. Fool or liar, the truth will soon come out and I shall be shamed, hurt and rejected.' So you mustn't have anything to do with fools and liars!

Where you place yourself on your 'How I feel about myself' dimension depends on the judgements you make about yourself on certain values or virtues.

The judgements you make about yourself you also make about other people.

The higher you place yourself on your 'How I feel about myself' dimension the easier you are in your judgements about yourself and other people.

The lower you place yourself on your 'How I feel about myself' dimension the harder you are in your judgements about yourself and other people.

For instance, like most of us you might have accepted your parents' teaching that one important aspect of being good is to work hard. So you judge yourself and other people on how hard you and they work.

However, the more you value and accept yourself, the more likely you are to temper your judgement of yourself and others with ideas like, 'I've worked hard all day. Now I'm going to put my feet up and watch television,' and 'It doesn't matter how busy you are, you must take a proper holiday.'

The less you value and accept yourself the more likely you are to be harsh in your judgements of yourself and others. If you watch television you feel guilty for wasting time, and you condemn friends and colleagues for not keeping their homes immaculate or for wanting to go on holiday.

It's in these condemnatory judgements of other people that the meaning structure's pride in itself is revealed.

Your meaning structure, being a living structure, is in the business of survival. The purpose of life is to live. It doesn't matter how much you denigrate yourself, how much you tell yourself you don't deserve to exist, your meaning structure intends to go on surviving and will do so using a strategy which we know as pride.

So there you are telling yourself what a wicked, contemptible person you are, and even as you are doing so, you are taking pride in the fact that you know that you are wicked and contemptible, while all those other people are as wicked and contemptible as you are but they don't recognize that they are and so don't feel the shame and guilt which they should feel. Whereas you do feel shame and guilt, which shows that you are good, and better than other people. So your meaning structure, taking pride in itself, survives.

Enjoying such proud humility is a very popular pastime.

The pride you take in your humility prevents you from having easy, happy relationships with other people. Such pride makes you lonely, but then you can take pride in your loneliness. You keep yourself to yourself.

There are many people who seem to be full of self-confidence and enjoying good relationships but are doing so only because they have carefully structured their lives so that they always stay in the same place, meet the same people and follow the same set of rules, day after day, year after year. The places, people and rules are like a hard, protective shell while the person hides inside, a quivering jelly, afraid to venture out. Such a hard shell can consist of the routines of those families which the media call (in praise) 'close-knit' as well as the rules and customs that different class, national, religious or racial groups adhere to so fiercely.

The quivering jellies within these hard shells maintain the integrity of their meaning structures by the strength of their prejudices against those people whom they exclude from their lives and whom they are too frightened to encounter at all or only in very structured ways.

Living in such a way these people deprive themselves of the joys of encountering an amazing variety of people, thus enlarging their own meaning structure. They add to their suffering and the suffering of others by maintaining those divisions which have been the source of the cruelty, devastation and war which throw into question whether we are the most intelligent species that this planet has yet seen.

Moreover, such people place themselves at risk of running out of enough people to help them maintain themselves and save them from loneliness.

If you are one of those people who insist that you live in the same place, mix with the same people and follow the same set of rules year after year, all you have to do to be quite alone is to fall out with your children and wait for your contemporaries to die.

Perhaps you are not such a person. Perhaps you have regained much of the self-confidence with which you were born.

But no matter how consistently you place yourself high on your 'How I feel about myself' dimension, you will still find it difficult to have good relationships with people who consistently place themselves low on theirs. You find that people who don't think much of themselves aren't very good at understanding you and so your relationships with them are often very fraught.

The lower your opinion of yourself, the more you consistently place yourself low on your 'How I feel about myself' dimension, the more you worry about being good yet, ironically, the more self-absorbed and selfish you will become.

You are so busy worrying about what other people think about you that you have no time to notice what they are actually doing and feeling. If you did notice you might find that they weren't thinking about you at all. Oh, perish the thought!

(There are many people who prefer to be paranoid rather than to be ignored.)

This self-absorption means that you don't spend time observing other people and learning about how they interpret the world. Although you don't want to hurt people, out of your ignorance of them you do hurt and annoy them by what you say and do. When they react in pain and anger you become confused and feel put upon and maltreated.

You protest with, 'What did I say?' and 'Why don't people like me?'

These are rhetorical questions. You don't want to be told anything other than you are right and other people wrong. You don't want to lose any of the pleasure you find in taking things personally (another form of your meaning structure's strategy of maintaining itself in the face of adversity by resorting to pride).

It is so easy to explain other people's hurtful reactions to you by saying, 'That person doesn't like me.'

It is much more difficult and time consuming to:

1. realize that in relationships you are encountering meaning structures whose interpretations are very different from your own
2. take these other meaning structures seriously and treat them with respect
3. learn how to listen and to ask effective questions in order to discover and understand these other meaning structures.

(Effective questions are appropriate versions of 'How do you feel about that?', 'Why is that important to you?' and 'Would I be right in thinking that this is how you feel about something or see something?')

Yet it is only by making such an effort that you can be reasonably accurate in understanding why people behave as they do and therefore predict what they might do in a given situation.

Living with someone whose feelings and actions you can't predict is very scary. How can you persuade someone to do what you want them to do if you don't know what they are thinking?

Over the past decade or so many business leaders have come to realize that to sell their product they need to know how their potential customers interpret the product and its place in the world. Yet it seems that many of the business people involved in such marketing techniques don't realize that these techniques might even more usefully be applied to the rest of their relationships with colleagues, friends and family.

I was once talking to a very senior manager of an international car company who was telling me about the company's plan to re-position one range of their cars in a special market. The research for this programme involved, amongst other things, asking a large sample of people to respond to the question, 'If each of these cars were a person, what sort of person would it be?' When I commented that this form of question was also used in therapy by Personal Construct psychologists like myself, the manager looked most disconcerted. How could business techniques have anything to do with real life?

Yet what this marketing research was doing was something which we all ought to do in our relationships. Rather than nag, whine, threaten, get angry or feel bitterly disappointed when someone fails to do what you want, begin by determining whether the person is capable of acceding to your request.

Just because a person is physically capable of carrying out an action does not mean that the person's meaning structure has the requirements to carry out that action. Meaning structures have boundaries. Whether you will do what I want you to do depends on what lies within your meaning structure's boundaries.

Suppose I wanted to persuade you to take up yoga for the good of your health.

If your meaning structure already contains structures like, 'Exercise always makes me feel better,' or 'I'm always keen to try new things' there's a good chance that you'll accept what I say.

But if your meaning structure contains structures like, 'I wouldn't be seen dead in a leotard,' or 'Yoga is a manifestation of the devil' (a structure which is held by many of the more fundamentalist clergy) it's unlikely you'll take my advice.

All this seems obvious, but nevertheless some people spend, and ruin, their lives waiting for their nearest and dearest to behave in a way which actually lies right outside the nearest and dearest's meaning structure.

A woman's dissatisfaction with her marriage might be based on her desire that her husband prove his love for her in romantic ways, yet he doesn't know and doesn't want to know what the word 'romantic' means. He suspects it means, when applied to men, 'weak and effeminate'.

A man might wait all his life for his father to reveal his pride in his son's achievements, while the father, envious of the son's achievements, believes that the only worthwhile achievements are his own.

Exploring another person's meaning structure can be very disturbing. Other people's interpretations throw doubt on your own. (This is why authoritarian governments, religions and families maintain censorship.)

It is disturbing too when you discover that other people's meaning structures can change. Have you noticed that whenever your meaning structure has changed significantly, even if the change means that you are happier and more fulfilled, some, if not all of your loved ones, are not pleased. They want you to stay the same so that when they do have to think about you they don't have to think anything other than what they have always thought.

Understanding other people is hard work, yet, if you don't make the effort, you miss out on those wonderful experiences which dissolve

*the barriers which you and others have constructed and thus
lessen the aloneness of our individual lives.*

It is curious that such experiences so often come, not in sharing joy and happiness, but in sharing sorrow. It seems that the
shared recognition of the tragedy of our lives which is our
helplessness in an unpredictable world, indifferent to our existence, brings us together so that we can recognize and bear our
tragic helplessness. Terrible disasters like the deaths of spectators
at Hillsborough Football Ground or the loss of life with the
sinking of the P & O ferry *Herald of Free Enterprise* brought
people from diverse backgrounds into the closest of friendships.

Friends with whom we have shared our sorrows and our joys
become part of our meaning structure, part of our life story. If
ever you have lost through death a long-time friend you'll know
how it feels as if part of you has gone.

When my friend Jean Flanagan died I was distressed not just
because we could not continue a conversation which started
thirty-three years ago. Jean and I, as young wives married to
men who were Australian larrikins (or so they liked to think),
shared much drama. Jean knew things about me which no one
else knew, and now that knowledge has gone. Part of me, my
story, has vanished.

We ought, as children, to be taught how to create and cherish
friendships. Knowing how to make people feel welcome, how
to remember what is important to other people, how to receive
generously and not just give, how to maintain a continuing
conversation despite separations are all skills which have to be
learnt.

If you are born to parents who cherish friendships you can
learn these skills by copying your parents. You learn that friends
need your time, energy and consideration. However, if you're
born to parents who exclude most of the human race from their
home, making and keeping friends are skills which as a child
you do not see, much less learn. In later life you need to discover
that you lack these skills and set about acquiring them if you
are to have satisfactory friendships.

Alas, there are many people who reserve their friendship skills
only for people outside the family. Within the family they

behave appallingly. The family becomes a group of victims and victimizers. They alternate the roles. The long-suffering mother terrorizes her children through guilt, the siblings bully and are bullied by one another, the bullied children bully their ageing father as he loses power.

If you're born to parents who treat you and your siblings as friends, you grow up having siblings as friends. However, if you're born to parents who do not treat you as a friend and who do not show you and your siblings that you should treat one another as friends, not as jealous enemies, in adult life you can find it very difficult to turn siblings into friends. In families a shared history can get in the way of friendship.

Not knowing how to be a friend, you don't know how to turn a lover into a friend. A passionate love affair can be great fun and make you feel you haven't wasted your life, but passion alone cannot sustain a relationship. Only friendship can do that.

You need friendships not just to maintain your existence or your sanity. You need friendships to enhance and enlarge your experiences by allowing you to see your experiences not only through your own interpretations but through other people's. You need friends to take you into other worlds of meaning. That way your life becomes large and various, not narrow and mean.

Sartre was right when he said that hell is other people. But so is heaven.

CHAPTER 11

You and Emotion

EMOTION is meaning.

Unfortunately, many philosophers, psychologists, psychiatrists and therapists haven't realized this. They divide our experience into cognition (thoughts) and emotion (often called 'affect') and then argue which comes first and which causes which. Such theorizing ignores our actual experience. Suppose you're walking along a street when a huge dog leaps a fence and, barking and slavering, bounds towards you. Thinking 'I'm in danger' and feeling frightened are one and the same experience. Of course, in trying to understand our experiences we can divide our thoughts from our feelings, but such a division cannot replicate our actual experience any more than studying a container of hydrogen and a container of oxygen will give us an experience of water.

Cognitions are not the only meanings which we construct. They are simply the meanings we have constructed which come into clear consciousness and are expressed in words. Many of the meanings we construct we never express in words. We construct many meanings before we have a language to express them in, and even after we acquire language we continue to construct meanings in the way we always have, in images and feelings.

These images can be pictures, or sounds, or smells, or tastes, or touch, or kinaesthetic images. (The last are images of our body moving or being acted upon in some way. Try, without moving, to create an image of how it feels to hold a cricket bat or put on lipstick.) Feelings can be the relatively simple ones like love, hate, fear, anger, aggression, envy, jealousy, guilt, shame, regret, sadness, joy, delight and enthusiasm. Languages differ in what they recognize and name as emotions. German uses the same word for 'guilt' and 'debt', while Japanese, very usefully, has a word for 'regret for feeling regret'. Frequently what we feel is a combination of certain emotions in all kinds of degrees. Love and delight go together as do fear and hate. Often a pair of felt emotions conflict with one another. My friend Lou, who liked to be liked, found herself very much liked by a man she despised.

Because our meaning structure and our body is one whole, the processes of creating meaning and of bodily changes happen together. The amount of bodily changes in the creation of some meanings can be very small, whereas in the creation of other meanings the bodily changes can be extensive.

Meanings which are accompanied by noticeable bodily changes are usually called emotions or feelings, although we do use the language of emotions when few bodily changes are present, as in, 'I love ice-cream.'

There are no specific sets of bodily changes which relate directly to each emotion. There is one set of bodily changes – increase in level of adrenalin, increasing heart and breathing rate and increase in sweating – which at times we call fear, at other times pleasurable excitement, and at other times sexual attraction. The common factor is that, in the creation of a meaning about danger, pleasure or sex, all these meanings require us to spring into some kind of action. This particular set of bodily changes gets us ready to do just that.

Many of the meanings we create do not become conscious. Thus you can see a situation in such a way that you create a meaning, 'I'm frightened' but not be consciously aware of being afraid. If you feel a bit shaky (the effect of the adrenalin) you can interpret this as being excited or as having a cold coming on. If you do acknowledge that you are frightened you can then create a meaning to explain the cause of your fear. For this you have a multitude of choices.

Regrettably, just as many people don't understand that emotion is always a meaning, many don't understand that emotion is always a response to something in our situation.

For nearly ten years I have been answering readers' letters in the magazine *Chat*. Readers write to me about family problems. The letters I receive are many and various, but most of them take the form of 'My child is bad. How do I make him good?'

Almost the entire letter is taken up with a description of the child's behaviour. Young children have temper tantrums. Older children are aggressive, moody and steal and lie. All are cheeky and disobedient.

Some of the letters run to several closely written pages and some are short, but all are devoted to a minute description of the child's behaviour. So qualified is the description that there is not a shred of information about the situation the child is in, except perhaps in passing. A letter might begin with, 'I am a single mother' or contain a glimpse of family life as in 'He is worse during the week when his father is away'.

What these letters reveal is that the writers believe that their child's bad behaviour is generated solely by the child. The bad behaviour is seen as a problem for the parents but not as the child's response to the parents' behaviour. The behaviour is not seen as the way the child is expressing the emotions of anger, fear, loss, guilt, shame, jealousy, envy or resentment but simply as evidence that the child is naughty, bad, even wicked.

In answering the letter I usually ask the writer to look at herself.

'Do you ever feel an emotion come over you all by itself like rain falling out of a clear sky? Sometimes it feels like that, but if you watch yourself carefully you'll find that every emotion, pleasant or unpleasant, comes into being in response to something in your situation. You love someone, or get frightened of someone, or get angry with someone, or feel guilty about something and so on.'

I hope I have encouraged at least some of my readers to discover that every emotion they feel arises in response to something. It might be a memory or an anticipation or something happening in the present, but whatever, an emotion is always a response. A response is always the creation of meaning. It might be an emotion in response to an object (as when you kick the car because it won't start) or, more usually, in response to something another person has said or done. So I advise my readers,

If you want to know why a child behaves as he does, look at the situation that child is in.

This applies to adults as well as children.

You can try in imagination putting yourself in another person's situation. However, this is only a guess and you can be wildly wrong.

The only way to find why a person behaves as he does is to ask him. If he trusts you he will tell you.

Alas, most children learn very early not to trust their parents. They know that if they tell their parents what they feel the parents will tell them that they are silly, or stupid, or wicked to feel such things.

Children also learn not to bring to the parents' attention something which the parents want to ignore. Parents often don't want to be reminded that the child is interpreting what the parents do.

A child's behaviour is not a consequence of what the parents do. A child's behaviour is a consequence of how the child interprets what the parents do.

The emotions we feel are not directly a consequence of what other people do. They are a consequence of how we interpret what other people do.

Lou wrote to me about how she had interpreted her parents' behaviour,

Watching three angry people, my parents and my sister, locked in the same repeated patterns of conflict, I drew the conclusion as a child that, within intimate relationships, anger got you nowhere, was a breakdown in communication, and was best circumvented by going straight to the cause of the conflict and discussing kindly and calmly how things could be resolved. I'm still looking for the grown-up who prefers to do it that way too! And of course, in the meantime, I have been working on deconstructing the myth that I learned from my very powerful parents, that if I do anything to anger somebody, that person will utterly despise and reject me forever. It's interesting to see how the tools we use can help or hinder. For instance, it was certainly my sense of humour and appreciation of black comedy that got me through and helped me understand them, and me. But too much of that bemused detachment also helped me to put up with bad things in my subsequent relationships for far too long, and stopped me realizing that I didn't have to go on trying to understand and forgive and love the unforgivable and unlovable, and in actual fact, I could just bugger off and leave them to their misery.

Many people, like Lou, are born into families where the parents cannot cope with any expression of anger by their children. Such parents have not understood that anger is as natural to us as breathing and somehow we have to work out effective ways of dealing with our anger and the anger of other people. Forbidding any expression of anger is not effective, except in creating misery.

Anger is our natural response to frustration. When something gets in our way we are frustrated. A burst of anger can often enable us to break through whatever is holding us back. When I was an undergraduate I drove a 1936 Essex utility which frequently refused to start. However, it did respond very well to a kick, probably because the time I took to get out of the car, kick it and get back in was the time the over-full carburettor took to empty.

Perhaps you know all this, but I'm saying this just in case you're one of those people who've come to believe that anger is wicked and unnatural, as you are likely to have done if your parents always punished you for getting angry.

I've discovered that there are many people like this. At the height of the threat of nuclear war in the early eighties I wrote a book called *Living with the Bomb: Can We Live without Enemies?* The answer to this question is yes, because by having enemies outside our group we manage to live more peacefully within our group. (I'm not recommending this, just observing

what we do.) In my lectures on how there will always be wars
until we change how we organize our groups and bring up our
children I would talk about how anger and aggression are part
of our nature. After every lecture various people devoted to the
cause of world peace would advance on me furiously, declaring,
'How dare you say that I am aggressive! I am never aggressive!'

Of course I had given them good cause to be angry. What I
said threatened their whole meaning structure. The fear they
felt soon turned to anger.

Getting angry when we are frightened can help us survive. It can help keep us alive and hold our meaning structure together.

When we are children and our parents punish us for getting angry we cannot give up feeling angry any more than we can give up breathing. So we become angry by devious means.

Some people go on getting angry but foolishly lie to themselves, telling themselves they don't feel angry, only frightened. This is a popular ploy with extraverts to whom the expression of anger could create the greatest threat of all. Lou had to discover that what she had believed was an Absolute Truth of the Universe, 'If I do anything to anger somebody, that person will utterly despise and reject me forever' (and what better way to anger someone than to get angry?), was actually a myth.

Or rather, a relative truth. There are people who base their lives on the principle that if anyone offends them they never speak to that person again. They should be pitied, not feared, for they end up very lonely. The mother of a friend of mine has followed this policy all her life and, now in her sixties, she talks to no one except her daughter and then usually in terms of complaint and criticism. My friend fears (and hopes) that one day she too will become one of the unforgiven.

When we are children we need to discover ways of dealing with our anger because even if our parents can cope with our anger our teachers and other adults can't.

If you are wise you don't lie to yourself about your anger. You acknowledge your anger and undertake the work of creating a variety of ways of expressing your anger and identifying the appropriate situations in which to use them.

You might work out something similar to what follows in this list of ways to express anger.

1. Explosion of anger with shouting, swearing and throwing things.

To use this method you need to have discovered that all emotions, pleasant and unpleasant, are self-limiting, something which people who are afraid to express their anger don't always know. You can't go on raging and raging for ever, any more than you can go on laughing for ever.

As a solo performance a burst of shouting, swearing and throwing things is immensely satisfying, provided you don't break anything you value and there's no one within earshot. This method can also be extremely effective with family, colleagues and students, provided you do it only once and with excellent justification. Repeat performances make the recipients of your anger either fear and hate you or regard you as a fool.

2. Silence, but accompanied by a sharp intake of breath, sudden pallor (much more effective than heart-attack red) and a tightening of the lips. Slight tremor of the hands for added effect.

This performance doesn't help your feelings much, so you might need to go somewhere private and scream, but well performed it can strike terror and get you what you want. Never disclose what the dread consequences might be if you were to lose your temper but imply that these would be horrendous beyond imagination and utterly irretrievable.

Resist the temptation to be a martyr or to sulk. These ploys drive people away from you, either because they can't cope with their feelings of guilt or because they've got better things to do than worry about you.

3. The calm, reasoned discussion.

If you want to engage in a co-operative venture of a calm, reasoned discussion ending in a mature compromise, like Lou, you'll still be looking for the grown-up who prefers it that way. However, if you want to win such a discussion, you need to prepare your arguments beforehand. Always begin by capturing the high moral ground. Say, 'I want to share my feeling of anger with you.' Speak in tones of pity, not anger.

There is one person with whom you can have a calm, reasoned discussion – yourself, when you've finished screaming. Work out exactly what the frustration/threat is and what to do about it. Would a good sleep get things back into proportion for you? Order your priorities. Is being seen to be good by yourself and others at the top of your priorities (which means you'll put up with the unlovable and the unforgivable even if it kills you, which it probably will)? Or should you just bugger off and leave the unlovable and unforgivable to their misery?

4. *The letter (or fax).*

Use this when the recipient of your anger might not be prepared to see you face to face or where you feel that in a face to face encounter you might not be able to control your emotions. Killing someone or beating someone up doesn't in the long run advance your cause. Women who in confrontations try to suppress their murderous impulses often find themselves bursting into tears, thus putting themselves in a very weak position.

Working out what you're going to put in the letter can be an immensely pleasurable expression of your own anger. Sometimes just writing the letter and not sending it is enough for you, especially if the consequences of sending the letter would be ones which you don't want. Letters written late at night shouldn't be sent until they have been re-read in the cold light of day.

Writing a letter can be a skill which, like me, you can hone into a fine art. My one-time husband once advised the world at large, 'Never put yourself in a situation where she can write you a letter.' He should know.

5. *Humour.*

How has the physically puny human race survived catastrophic disasters, their own stupidity and the total uncertainty of life? By humour.

Humour can exist only when there is uncertainty and imperfection. In the perfection of heaven there can be no humour, just as humour isn't possible for those people who insist that everything is exactly the way they say it is. Dictators, political and domestic, are against humour.

With a joke you can get away with murder. Hence the popularity of black comedy and cartoons that rely on *Schadenfreude*, the joy we take in another person's discomfiture. But sometimes you have to keep your joke to yourself and use it to express your anger and cheer yourself up. The object of your humour might not always respond in a way you find satisfactory.

This is the problem with anger. You can learn to accept your own anger and develop a set of flexible responses, but how do you deal with other people's anger?

Here are some suggestions:

1. Take it personally.

'Taking it personally' means that you have decided that you and you alone are both the cause and the object of the other person's anger and that this is unjust because, even if your actions have caused the other person's problems, you meant well. Moreover, you are a sensitive person, easily hurt by another person's uncaring behaviour. 'Taking it personally' means that you never see that in some situations the other person is not angry with you at all but at the institution for which you are nothing but the representative or messenger. In both situations you have a good reason for taking the other person's anger personally. In the first you are trying to avoid all responsibility for your actions and in the second you are trying to inflate your power and importance by claiming total responsibility. Both responses are a refusal to analyse carefully what is happening in that particular situation. You prefer to jump to the lazy conclusion, 'That person hates me.'

No matter if the person was directing his anger at someone else or just letting off steam, by taking it personally you increase your self-importance. You are a victim. Other people should pity you and look after you, even if you did provoke the anger in the first place. By taking it personally you can sometimes force the other person to do what you want, but don't kid yourself that that makes the other person like you and want to be close to you.

Moreover, taking it personally does make you feel miserable as you creep away to examine your wounds.

2. *Get angry and respond with great vigour.*

Shouting and throwing things at the person who's angry with you can be immensely satisfying, but there is always the danger that in the heat of the moment you'll say things that later you wish you hadn't. In anger, as *in vino*, truth, as you see it at that moment, will out.

If, as a couple, you frequently fight like this, your friends and family will come to expect you to liven up a dull party or dinner with a performance. They then get most put out if you take yourselves off to a counsellor where you discover that you weren't fighting over anything real but only differing interpretations of events. You no longer have any reason to fight, thus giving friends and family nothing to gossip about.

3. *Being tremendously reasonable while implying that the other person is completely unreasonable in being angry with you.*

This method is war by other means. Used against someone you'll never meet again it can leave you feeling a winner (please don't bore people with the story), but if you use it against family, friends and colleagues they'll keep on fighting you and you'll eventually succumb to their attrition or else they'll tire of trying to get you to understand their point of view. They'll leave you alone and lonely.

4. *Taking the other person's anger seriously.*

This is hard work. First you have to accept that in the here and now this is what the person feels (even if it's your sweet little three-year-old screaming, 'I hate you, Mummy!). You don't run away from this anger, nor are you affronted, nor do you belittle it. Then you have to search for the causes of the person's anger and ascertain what degree of responsibility you have for those causes. Finally you have to decide what you might appropriately do. Is it a matter of just letting the person express his anger, or of apologizing and making amends, or of getting out of the situation and keeping yourself safe?

All this is much easier to do when you have put yourself high on your 'How I feel about myself' dimension. When you're low on that dimension every attack on you, however unjustified, plunges you lower and you find personal responsibility and guilt wherever you look. You feel that you anger people just by existing.

5. *Revenge*.

Revenge is an act of pride carried out by the meaning structure in order to preserve its integrity. 'Getting your own back' means getting back to the state of your meaning structure which prevailed before you were attacked.

A simple example:

I'm driving down the motorway in the fast lane at ninety miles per hour. I pass a sales executive dawdling along in his Granada. Suddenly he realizes that he has been passed by a grey-haired woman in an old Golf CL. His whole meaning structure, whose 'How I feel about myself' dimension is devoted to being a manly chap, is under threat. He swings into the outside lane and comes after me with headlights flashing. I know there's nothing more dangerous on a motorway than a decomposing meaning structure, so I pull over and let him pass. A few miles on he's back dawdling in the middle lane, his meaning structure still intact.

Do I whizz by with a cheery wave, urging him on to another act of revenge, or hang back and make myself late? Neither option appeals. Usually I wait until he drifts into the slow lane and I pass him with the cover of a truck, or else I go by in a closely spaced stream of traffic. Either ploy preserves my meaning structure and avoids a stupid game of revenge.

Revenge carried out as destruction and death always leads to defeat and continuing suffering. Today's news, whatever day it is, will furnish a plethora of examples. Revenge carried out in the spirit of humour achieves what the meaning structure needs to achieve and without continuing suffering, or at least no more suffering than the jokes in return engender.[9]

Sometimes the desire for revenge arises solely out of anger and sometimes the anger is mixed with the hatred which arises out of jealousy.

The words 'envy' and 'jealousy' are often used interchangeably, but you can think more clearly about these matters if you keep the meaning of the two words distinct.

Envy is what we feel when we want something which someone else has.

Jealousy is what we feel when someone has something which we see as rightly ours.

Thus in a family the older child might envy the younger one for the toys she has been given for her birthday but feel jealous of the younger child because he feels that she has taken the mother's love which is rightly his.

Often such jealousy is a cover for the anger and hatred which a person dare not acknowledge even to himself.

Imagine being an only child, the centre of your parents' universe. You bask in their love. Then one day your mother disappears and reappears with a new baby. You're displaced and you're angry.

With whom? Your mother of course. She has betrayed you. You find your mother pushing you aside and giving her attention to the baby.

You realize that if you turn your anger on your mother she might send you away for ever. You know you can't manage without her. So you daren't be angry with her. Instead you turn your anger on to the baby. How dare that baby take what is rightfully yours!

Yet you know, though you won't let yourself know that you know, that the cause of your misery is not the baby. From then on, no matter what your mother does to please you it is never enough. You will never forgive her. You will never let her off the hook.

And of course you are also caught by the same hook, especially as you get older and you discover that your jealousy brings you a great reward. Never again will you have to blame yourself for any of your failures. You can tell yourself that every failure, every disaster has been caused by the existence of the sibling your mother preferred to you.

Another situation you might like to imagine is that of the lover who discovers that his partner is unfaithful. (The lover might just as easily be a she and the partner a he or a she.) Instead of being very angry with your faithless lover you become intensely jealous of the new lover.

Friends who find your behaviour odd don't realize that your jealousy is a cover for the anger you feel with your lover. However, you daren't express or even acknowledge to yourself this anger lest you lose your partner completely. You believe that your partner is indispensable to your life. Lose your partner and your meaning structure (or so it seems to you) will fall apart.

As the child or as the lover such hidden anger in the guise of jealousy keeps you trapped. You can't let go of the past and the present refuses to conform to your wishes. You can't be free until you acknowledge that you are angry, whom you are angry with and why. Such acknowledgement might, one day, allow forgiveness to arise.

Forgiveness isn't a feeling which you can will into existence. Like every emotion it can come into being only when the necessary meanings are present in your meaning structure.

The meanings necessary for forgiveness are:

1. The offence, whatever it was, is no longer important to you.
2. You can see and to some extent accept how the perpetrator saw the situation. (Becoming a parent yourself can certainly help in coming to forgive your parents.)
3. You have come to feel that the injury you suffered did have some beneficial effects for you or some of the people you care about.
4. You have nothing to lose if you forgive.

When these meanings are in place you find that forgiveness is not so much an actively felt emotion as a letting go. It is a sense of release, of freedom, of doors opening, of going forward.

Some people very soon after the harmful act was committed claim that they have forgiven those who have harmed them. Sometimes this is done because the person wants to think of himself as a good person. He does not want to unleash the rage which might show him to be as evil as his transgressors (he is afraid of anger and thinks it wicked), nor does he want to feel guilty for failing to forgive. Sometimes the act of public forgiveness is merely a seizure of the high moral ground as an act of retribution against the transgressors ('My virtue shows just how wicked you are!') This can be satisfying and effective, so long as you don't kid yourself that you really have forgiven.

Because we're always having Christian forgiveness preached at us many people feel guilty because they can't forgive. But if you haven't arrived at the necessary meanings you are demanding something from yourself which is beyond your capacity to perform.

If you are finding that you cannot forgive a certain offence ask yourself the following questions:

1. Do you feel that by forgiving you lose something of yourself and so feel weaker? Have you placed yourself low on your 'How I feel about myself' dimension and therefore feel the need to shore up your self-confidence by being hard, unforgiving and seeking revenge?
2. Is the offence still important to you because it was an attack on something very central to your meaning structure?
3. Have you not attempted to understand how the perpetrator saw the situation or, if you have done this, have you decided that the perpetrator acted with nothing but evil intent?
4. Do you feel that to forgive would be to lower your guard against someone who is likely to strike again?
5. Is the injury that has been done to you so gross that there have been no beneficial results other than that you now know how other people suffering similar injuries feel?

Perhaps in answering these questions you will come to see that if you valued yourself more you wouldn't need to trap yourself by refusing to forgive. Remember that not forgiving is an active process that takes up time and energy which could be used more productively elsewhere. Remember too that forgiving does not necessarily mean that you have to clutch the transgressor to your bosom in a loving embrace. In the process of establishing the meaning structures necessary for forgiveness you need to study the transgressor carefully. You might conclude that a certain protective distance, psychological and/or geographical, is necessary for your wellbeing.

This is an issue which often arises when you decide to embark on the journey of self-understanding.

Usually you are pushed into this journey by the painful feelings of unnameable fears and a sense of self-hate and self-disgust. On this journey you discover that you are not the loathsome, unacceptable person that you thought you were, but that you came to feel like this because of the way you interpreted your parents' behaviour when you were a small child.

Such a discovery makes you very angry with your parents. How dare they treat you like that!

If, by ill-fortune, you have fallen into the hands of an unscrupulous therapist who has helped you make this discovery you can spend the rest of your life being angry with your parents. You (and the therapist) turn what is an *explanation* for your situation into an *excuse*. You continue on in therapy, exploring every real and imagined instance where your parents failed to be everything you desired. You and your therapist now have a perfect relationship. You now have an excuse for your every failure and shortcoming and your therapist has a secure income.

However, if, by the greatest of good fortune, you have found a good therapist, he or she will leave you in no doubt that you have only just begun your journey. Such a therapist makes it clear to you that all you have is an explanation. It is not an excuse. Don't try saying, 'I can't help my bad behaviour. I had an unhappy childhood.' You'll be told that you're an adult now and, even though you can't control everything that happens to you, you do control and are responsible for how you interpret what happens to you.

A good therapist does not badger you into premature forgiveness as some sentimental therapists are prone to do but helps you explore to see if you can construct the meanings which are the necessary prerequisite for forgiveness.

Like many people on such a journey, you need to find out

more about the events of your childhood. Who better than your parents?

Thus a great many parents of adult children are finding themselves being asked to recall events of long ago. Sometimes the questions are simple. 'For how long was I breast-fed?' 'Did I cry much as a baby?' Sometimes the questions are hard, even harder than the questioner knows because they demand the recall of some very painful events.

Nowadays bad therapists often require their clients to confront their parents with their real or imagined errors. Such confrontations do not advance the client's wellbeing, though they do secure the therapist's wealth and power.

Good therapists do not tell their clients to approach, much less confront, their parents but if the client chooses to seek his parents' help the therapist then helps him to explore and surmount the consequences.

Some parents, lacking the self-confidence to admit any mistakes, are affronted by such questions. In doing so they prevent themselves from working out with their child a new relationship which reflects that the parent-child relationship is no longer appropriate but that friendship among adults is.

Other parents, glad of the opportunity to review the past, a task which they must carry out if they are to face their own deaths with any equanimity, talk to their children regardless of the pain this might re-awaken.

If you, as a parent of an adult child, find yourself in this situation, don't feel helpless because you cannot undo the past. If your child has come to you in the search for self-understanding and not in the search for an excuse for his failures, all you have to say is, 'Yes, these things happened. I'm sorry.'

This response secures the memories which are essential for a solid, self-accepting sense of self and joins you with your child in the most binding of all our emotions, a shared sense of sadness.

CHAPTER 12

You and Power

POWER ISN'T a force which some people have and some people don't. It isn't an attribute or possession.

Power is a relationship between the interpretations made by one person (the so-called 'powerful' one) and those made by other people. You can stand in front of your bathroom mirror and tell yourself, 'I am powerful', but if no one else agrees that you are powerful, you aren't. If you go on insisting to other people that you are powerful and no one agrees with you, you'll be called mad and dealt with accordingly.

To be powerful you have to have power over other people, but this can happen only if those people see you as having power over them. Suppose you came after me with a loaded gun and ordered me to do your bidding. If I believed that a loaded gun could kill me and if I didn't want to die (two interpretations I am quite likely to make) I would see you as having power over me. But if you came after me, not with a gun but with a political manifesto, and ordered me to believe what was in that manifesto, I would be completely unimpressed and so not give you any power at all.

Back in the early eighties when the danger of a nuclear war was at its height someone coined the slogan, 'What if they gave a war and nobody came.' If you give a party and nobody comes, there's no party. If you give a war and nobody comes, there's no war.

A simple way to end wars, but of course it didn't work. There are always many men who will give other men the power to order them to fight and die, and many men who are pleased to accept this power. Often these men labour under the delusion that they are in the possession of an Absolute Truth such as, 'My country is the greatest in the world' or 'My religion is the only true religion.' The people who always benefit from wars are not those who fight them but those who supply the weapons. They hold to another truth, 'Money is power'. In a capitalist society this statement is often treated as an Absolute Truth, but alone on a desert island with nothing but money you'll find that it isn't. Money, like power, is a relationship among interpretations made by different people. If these complementary relationships do not exist, money is no more than a lump of metal, a piece of paper, or figures on a computer screen.

To be powerful you have to be seen by other people as being powerful.

When you give someone the right to be powerful you're giving something intangible but very important. You're giving that person the right to impose his interpretations on you.

Power is the right to have your interpretations prevail over other people's interpretations.

Some people look as if they are powerful because they have the trappings of power but in fact they have not been given the right to impose their interpretations on other people. The Queen of England might, in her Christmas address, advise her subjects not to smoke, but with little effect because her subjects don't see her as having the power to impose her ideas on them. However, if Parliament passed a law ordering all smokers to be arrested, tried and sent to prison, or if the Chancellor of the Exchequer raised the tax on tobacco by a thousand per cent nicotine consumption in Britain would decrease because the British would see Parliament and its representatives as having the right to impose their interpretations on British citizens.

Unfortunately, many people don't understand that power is a set of reciprocal interpretations. They think that the power of the State and the Church is real and fixed. Some people see their parents' power or that of a doctor or a lawyer in the same way. Consequently all such people feel trapped and helpless.

If people see the power of their religion as absolute, total and

eternal they still feel themselves to be under the domination of this power even if they cease to carry out its rituals and believe its dogma. An elderly man I was talking to recently told me that he had left the Catholic Church in disgust and would never let a priest cross his threshold. A little while later he said he knew that his many illnesses were a punishment for his sins. Other lapsed Catholics remain enthralled by what the Church calls its mysteries and become annoyed if a non-religious person questions their validity. Of course, if a religion claims to hold absolute, total and eternal power it cannot allow followers to say that they have left it. The Catholic Church, so I'm told, has abandoned the word 'lapsed' in favour of 'resting'. Like a 'resting' actor waiting for the next play, a 'resting' Catholic will soon and inevitably awaken and return to the fold.

Many people see the institutions of the government and the law as absolute, total and eternal. They see no point in voting and they would sooner become a space traveller than join a political party. They have handed over power to the fallible men and women of the government and the law in the belief that 'they' will look after them. When 'they' fail to provide, they are most aggrieved.

My mother, like many people, gave doctors, lawyers and bank managers an absolute status of being in some way better than herself and her family and an absolute power over herself and her family. Such absolute status and power made her fearful of them. She avoided lawyers and bank managers and failed to consult doctors when it would have been in her interests and mine to do so.

In the course of my work I have met many people who see their parents as having absolute, total and eternal power. Even though they have been given evidence over and over throughout their lives that their parents are, like everyone else, fallible, weak human beings, they don't want to give up the hope that their parents are strong and wise enough to hold up the sky and keep them safe beneath. What they experience most often is not a sense of safety but their terror of such powerful people. They believe that if they err, their parents, near or far, alive or dead, will know and punish them.

Some people manage to abandon their belief in absolute, total and eternal power by discovering what is nowadays called 'empowerment'. This is simply coming to understand that, while we do have to accept that rain falls from the skies when it will, we don't have to accept the interpretations which other people seek to impose on us. It's not just that we have a right to our own point of view but that we can't have anything else other than our own point of view. This applies even when we have accepted what other people have told us is the correct point of view. (There are as many forms of Christianity as there are people who call themselves Christian.)

Being empowered means realizing that you do not have to interpret those who present themselves as being powerful as actually being powerful. Of course there are many situations where it would be wise to keep your 'empowered' thoughts to yourself. This is the perennial problem for all dictators, political or domestic. Thought is always private.

Thinking thoughts contrary to those desired by the would-be powerful people around you can be gratifying, but only to a certain degree. There comes a point where you must act on your private interpretations or else feel frustrated and begin to doubt the accuracy of your interpretations. You need to act on your interpretations in order to check just how true they are. As we've already discussed, to stay sane your meaning structure needs to be in as close a relationship as possible with what is going on around you.

Most often such checking involves comparing your interpretations with someone else's interpretations. The Prime Minister declares that the country's economy is booming. You think he is wrong. To check your interpretation you can ask other people what they think.

When someone disagrees with your interpretation you can

1) accept the other person's interpretation and give up your own

or

2) try to impose your interpretation on the other person.

(Agreeing to differ is just a polite way of deciding that the other person is an idiot.)

In (1) you have given power to the other person and in (2) you have tried to get power for yourself.

Sometimes it is wise or useful to let the other person's interpretation prevail. You might let their interpretation take precedence over yours, or you might give up your interpretation and accept that of the other person. However, if you did that all the time your meaning structure would soon be under the most terrible threat of all, that of dissolution. You have to resist many of the interpretations that other people thrust on you in order to preserve the integrity of your meaning structure. This is why children persist in holding views contrary to those of their parents, why advertising has such limited effect, and why prisoners apparently in the total power of their guards have to create some area in their daily lives where they and not the guards are in control.

Thus most of the time in your interactions with other people you are trying to impose your interpretations on them and to resist the interpretations which they seek to impose on you.

Living as a person is a matter of constantly seeking power and avoiding helplessness.

(The power you seek might be no more than ordering your children to eat the wholesome dinner you've prepared or deciding which television programmes the family will watch, but it is power none the less.)

Just how you go about seeking power and avoiding helplessness depends on where you have placed yourself on your 'How I feel about myself' dimension.

The higher you place yourself on your 'How I feel about myself' dimension the less you need power and the less you fear helplessness.

The lower you place yourself on your 'How I feel about myself' dimension the more you seek power and the more you fear helplessness.

Being high on your 'How I feel about myself' dimension means that you feel that your interpretations of what is going on are reasonably accurate. You know that they can't be a hundred per cent accurate because that isn't humanly possible, but you have confidence that when discrepancies between your interpretations and what is actually happening do appear you will be able to deal with them.

Having confidence in your own judgement means that you are sceptical of all people who claim absolute certainty about anything, but you don't feel that your whole meaning structure will crumble if someone is able to show you that some of your judgements are wrong. When other people thrust power on you, you accept it when it is appropriate (as in fulfilling the role of parent or boss) and refuse it when it is inappropriate (when others expect you to assume the responsibility which is rightly theirs). When you do accept power you enjoy using your skills but you do not delude yourself that you are the only person capable of fulfilling these tasks or that you know what is best for other people.

There are many people who present themselves as being high on their 'How I feel about myself' dimension but they don't behave as I've described because they are in fact acting a role in order to hide that dark, secret cellar of self-disgust within themselves.

Some of these people are well aware of the dangerous darkness that threatens them but they have learnt that a show of self-confidence is an effective defence. Others foolishly lie to themselves, telling themselves that they are the greatest and the best.

The first group can be identified by the doubt and despair they feel in private. Winston Churchill, inspiring a nation, dealt with his despair and depression through alcohol.

The second group can be identified by the curious inconsistencies in their presentation of themselves. (If you lie to yourself there are bound to be inconsistencies in your behaviour.) They may address their audiences in tones of utter certainty but in what they say and do they reveal some curious oddities. Margaret Thatcher would have us believe that she sprang fully formed from her father, like Athena from the head of Zeus, rather than acknowledge the role her mother played in her life. Usually such people are trying to prove something to somebody in their past. Margaret Thatcher seems to be trying to prove something to her father, perhaps that she is as good, if not better, than a son, while the dictators Stalin and Saddam Hussein, having endured childhoods of great cruelty, sought revenge by persecuting those whom they saw as being like their persecutors.

Whether or not you reveal yourself as having placed yourself low on your 'How I feel about myself' dimension, being in that position means that you doubt the accuracy of your interpretations. You might know what you *ought* to feel and think but you don't know what you *do* feel and think. You can admit

this to yourself or you can deny it by claiming that all your interpretations are totally accurate and that you are in possession of the Absolute Truth.

If you choose to acknowledge your uncertainty you are always filled with doubt and fear and you are impressed by everyone who seeks to impose their interpretations on you. You are constantly duped by liars and conned by proselytizers of all persuasions.

If you choose to deny your uncertainty you are terrified by dissent and seek to stamp it out. In both cases you live in fear that your meaning structure will be overwhelmed and will crumble.

What can you do?

You can try to seize power in order to hold yourself together. You can try to impose your interpretations on other people.

If you're always filled with fear and doubt you can seize the power of utter selfishness. You ignore the needs, wishes and feelings of those around you and you demand that they always acknowledge your needs, wishes and feelings and respond to you as you desire.

You achieve this by playing on your loved ones' guilt and need to be approved of and accepted. You become a public saint and a private tyrant. A martyr to illness (or at least hypochondria), you know that you can defeat any rebellion by reference to your favourite symptoms, or by making a suicide threat, or throwing a temper tantrum, or indulging in a prolonged sulk. As I know from personal experience, being on the receiving end of such treatment is so stressful that you'll accept the other person's imposition of power just to get some peace, and thus you undermine your own self-confidence. Love doesn't survive such treatment, though guilt and fear do.

Not everyone who places themselves low on their 'How I feel about myself' dimension has a family capable of being terrorized. If you can't get your loved ones to accept your power to impose your interpretations you can impose your very idiosyncratic interpretations on yourself and your environment.

This is one way of describing the behaviours which psychiatrists call mental illnesses. Phobic people interpret their experience in terms of fear, death, abandonment, rejection and annihilation, and see their environment as full of terrors. Obsessive-compulsive people interpret their experience in terms of danger and doubt, and see their environment in terms of disaster and defence. Depressed people interpret their experience in terms of isolation, guilt and punishment, and see their environment as empty and hostile. Manic people interpret their experience in terms of activity and fear, and see their environment as a stage for action. Schizophrenic people interpret their experience in terms of their very idiosyncratic fantasies and fears, and see their environment as full of special significance for them alone. Anorexic people interpret their experience in terms of fat, food and acceptance, and see their environment, including their body, as something to be ordered and controlled. All such people, believing that they are facing the annihilation of their self, hold fast to their interpretations, seek to impose them on others and resist all attempts to relieve them of the power to which they lay claim.

Trying to gain power in this way is never effective, whereas claiming total certainty can be remarkably effective, at least for a while. You can claim to be God, or the saviour of the nation, or the only person who knows how others should behave. Whatever, you have become one of the most dangerous people in the world – those who claim to know what is best for other people. When offered power you seize it greedily.

Why do we give other people power?

The first and very sensible reason is that at times in our lives we need to be looked after. Newborn babies are wise and helpless. They look for a face they can rely on to reappear and they give that face power.

If you're wise, as you get older you'll gradually take back the power that you gave your mother because as long as you're dependent on her you can't become an independent adult. Unfortunately the world is full of people who have reached physical maturity but are still children. They're still dependent on their parents, dead or alive, and on other people to whom they've given the power of parents. Many of these people don't want to free themselves. Some are waiting, longing, hoping for the day when their parents will declare their unconditional love for their child, something which the child believes is the only thing which can restore a sense of self-worth. Some are trapped by their belief in the Fifth Commandment, 'Honour thy father and mother so that thy days will be long in the land'. Criticize your parents and you're dead. Others so doubt their own value and ability that they feel utterly unable to face the world alone. All are obedient citizens, easily led.

If you're wise you might also be lucky and have parents whom you can go on trusting after you've taken back their right to power over you. You are now friends. Friends trust one another and respect one another's point of view. They don't have power over one another.

At different times in your life you'll give power to another person in order to meet some need. You'll give power to a doctor when you're ill, to a pilot when you need to fly. (People who are terrified of flying are so untrusting of the pilot that they cannot give him the power to be responsible for their safety.) In these instances the power you give should be clearly circumscribed. Doctors might know more than you about how the body functions but they are no better than anyone else in understanding why you do what you do.

The rules of society include the expectation that you will grant a number of people the right to decide your political and economic fate. Here you should yield as little power as possible. Don't throw your own power away with, 'All those politicians are the same. I don't bother to vote and I'd never join a political party.'

The second reason we give other people power is the tawdry one of putting on to other people the responsibility which is our own. How wonderful to be able to blame others for our own mistakes! But how can you learn from your mistakes if you don't begin by acknowledging them?

The third reason we give other people power is because we're afraid of them.

Sometimes we give people power over us because we love them and want them to love us, and this makes us fearful. We think that if we don't give them power over us they will be hurt, and then they'll punish and reject us. Often in American television dramas one character, usually a man, says to another character, usually a woman, 'I love you therefore you must do what I want,' or, more briefly, 'I love you. Trust me.' The woman looks grateful when instead she should say, 'Loving me does not give you the right to order me around.' How could she, since her parents had probably bamboozled her with this false argument all through her childhood in order to make her be obedient!

In our society many people have invested the notion of love with immense power. They assume that it doesn't matter if your mother made your childhood a nightmare or your lover has ruined your life; so long as they loved you, even if they never showed it in any way, shape or form, everything is all right. Somehow love has the power to recompense us fully for all our pain and suffering! If this really were so, we would all be immensely happy people because we received most of our pain and torment at the hands of those who loved us (or said they did).

Often we give people power over us because they threaten us. Sometimes the threat is physical and sometimes the threat is against the integrity of our meaning structure. Parents say to a child, 'If you're naughty we'll send you away,' and the child feels the terror of complete abandonment. A dictatorial entrepreneur tells his managing director, 'Obey me or you're fired,' and the managing director whose whole meaning structure is built on achievement in terms of money and position is terrified and obeys.

Often we fear and hand over power when there is no need to fear. If you know what is most important to you and irreplaceable and what is merely pleasant to have, you can reduce significantly the number of situations where people can terrorize you into handing them power.

Don't give other people power unless it is essential to do so. Think of your denial of others' power as being for their benefit. You don't want them to be corrupted by power!

Many people holding power can be seduced into thinking

"AND IF GRANTED ABSOLUTE POWER, I PROMISE NOT TO ABUSE IT. TRUST ME."[11]

that the interpretations they have created are superior to other people's interpretations, even that their interpretations are not mere interpretations but accurate statements about reality. They tell themselves that they are uncorrupted by power but they are lying.

One way of avoiding being corrupted by power is to remember that there is no power without responsibility. If you have the power to make decisions which affect the welfare of other people, 'being responsible' means making decisions which are in the interests of these other people and not just in your own interests. Just who these other people are can be debatable. Should a Chief Executive Officer put the shareholders' interests first, or those of the workers or the public? It is easy to use this notion of responsibility to justify your own advantages. Certain members of the aristocracy would have us believe that the onerousness of their paternalist responsibility to their servants and retainers far outweighs the delights of their power, prestige and wealth.

Power also corrupts when the holder of the power gives up trying to establish relationships through love and understanding and instead decides to control others by making them afraid. The powerful person can easily forget that fear drives out love. A feared ruler is not a loved ruler. 'The root of the word *hate* in Arabic is the same as that for *fear*.'[12] A feared parent is not a loved parent. Feeling guilty about your parents is not evidence that you love them. Guilt is fear of punishment, not a sign of love.

Delicious though power might be it always fails.

Even though power is the right to impose your interpretations on other people, this is not a process like stamping your ideas on another person's meaning structure. You present your interpretations, and then the other person interprets your interpretations.

The other person's interpretations are never the same as yours. You can set up a system of thought reform, as was done in Communist China, or you can root out and kill all heretics, or you can beat your children every time they fail to respond as you want, but, no matter. Other people will go on making their own interpretations, thinking their own thoughts, even when they are apparently obeying you, and no two people will create exactly the same interpretations.

This is the greatest problem of being a parent. Imagine that your three children are gathered around the dining table and, with their best interests at heart, you say, 'Eat your dinner.' One child interprets your order as, 'I'll do this because I want to show how good I am,' another thinks, 'I won't. I'm sick of being bossed around,' and the third child is lost in a daydream and didn't hear what you said.

Rather than making the vain attempt to get everyone to accept your views it is better to recognize that the desire for power is a fear of helplessness. Helplessness is an inescapable condition of our life, so to fear helplessness is to fear life.

We live in a universe which is indifferent to our existence. As the scientist John Gribbin said, 'It is now clear that the Universe has not been set up for our benefit, and that the existence of organic life-forms on Earth is simply a minor side-effect of an evolutionary process involving universes, galaxies and stars which actually favours the production of black holes.'[13]

Whistling in the dark, we can pretend that the universe was created for us and refuse to see that we are part of, not the reason for, the universe. We can pretend that we can control the universe when in fact we control very little of the world we live in.

Many of the grand schemes to modify the planet for people's benefit have failed, while those that do succeed bring unexpected and unwanted consequences. Electricity has brought us pop-up toasters and pollution. Some people want to believe that they can control their health by thinking the right thoughts. Certainly anxiety, despair, resentment and bitterness interfere with the efficient functioning of the immune system, thus making the body vulnerable to disease and impairment, but positive thinking alone cannot altogether stem the tide of old age, infirmity and death.

The events which impinge on us arise from a vast network of events spreading all around the world and way back in time. We cannot control them. There is only one part of our existence over which we have choice and control.

We can choose and control how we interpret events.

Our choice is not limitless because we can choose only from our past experiences. However, we can limit our choices by limiting our experiences or we can choose to make our experiences as wide as possible by opening ourselves to the breadth of interpretations available from a diverse range of people.

If we do the second we can discover, as has been discovered by many people before us, that to deny our helplessness by claiming power serves only to increase our helplessness simply because we do not acknowledge the conditions of our existence. Whereas by acknowledging and accepting our helplessness we actually acquire the confidence in ourselves which renders power over others unnecessary.

CHAPTER 13

Is It All Your Fault?

I SOMETIMES THINK that all people can be divided into two groups – those who are responsible for nothing and those who are responsible for everything. There are those cabinet ministers and captains of industry who claim all the credit when their policies or their firms do well but when their policies or their firms inflict disaster on a helpless populace they say, 'It was nothing to do with me.' Then there are those people who, when their small children suffer from medical neglect or ignorance, when their adult children choose disastrous careers, when the firm they work for goes bankrupt, when scientists foretell the future of the planet in terms of doom and disaster, always cry, 'It's all my fault. I feel so guilty.'

I have to remind myself that there is another group of people, albeit small, who know that the question of who is responsible for what can never have a simple, one-or-the-other answer. They know that when you ask, 'Is it all my fault?' the correct answer always is,

Your responsibility for what happens to you and to other people varies from one situation to another, but you are always responsible for how you interpret what happens.

Determining the degree of responsibility for what happens requires careful thought. Many people have difficulty in doing this because when they were children they weren't helped to understand the concepts involved in determining responsibility.

Instead, the adults who should have helped them lied to them.

Did you have parents who told you that you were responsible for events the blame for which could not possibly be laid at your door? Were you told that eating all your dinner somehow benefited the starving children of Africa (or China, if you're my generation)? Were you told that by being good you prevented your mother from becoming ill? Or worse, were you told that if you had been really good your father wouldn't have left the family? Young and innocent of the devious ways of adults, you could do no other than believe them.

When you got to an age where your parents and teachers no longer felt that they had to be with you all the time, were you now told by them that you had to be 'responsible'? When you were punished for being 'irresponsible' did you realize that when the adults ordered you to be responsible they didn't mean you to be really responsible, that is, making your own decisions about the appropriate actions to take. They meant, 'Do what I want you to do even when I'm not there to see that you're being obedient.'

Did you find that instead of helping you to work out how to apportion blame they simply blamed you for everything? It didn't matter whether you had deliberately smashed your mother's best vase or whether you accidentally dropped it when you were trying to be helpful, you were blamed. When you broke your mother's vase and she flew into a rage and hit you, did she later say, 'I should have put it where you couldn't reach it' and 'I shouldn't have been so angry,' or did she say, 'It's your fault. You made me angry'?

Of course, being blamed unreasonably teaches you how to be unreasonable when you blame other people. This way you can deny that you are responsible for anything. You can go into therapy, discover that in your childhood your parents treated you badly and that this bad treatment made you feel bad about yourself. Doing this you can ignore the fact that feeling bad about yourself is not something which your parents inflicted on you but is the result of your interpretation of what your parents did.

Being unreasonable means that you can blame your parents for your misery just as they blamed you for theirs. You can ignore the fact that you're not responsible for what your parents did but you are responsible for how you interpret what they did, while your parents are responsible for what they did but not for how you interpret what they did.

This is all too complicated and seems to imply that you have to be responsible for what you do. Much better to stick to something simple. You can blame your parents for all your troubles and all your bad behaviour.

On the other hand, if you want to be wise you will always remember that

An explanation is not an excuse.

The fact that your parents treated you badly does not give you the right to behave badly, even though those addicts of all persuasions who are 'in recovery' and those people busy nurturing their upset 'inner child' claim that it does. Handing yourself over to a 'higher power' or claiming special dispensation for your 'inner child' are not examples of being responsible for yourself. Rather they are the egotistical manoeuvrings of someone who has not tried to understand what responsibility means.

When you were a child did the adults help you to work out that 'responsible' has two meanings? There's 'responsible' meaning 'cause' ('A blood clot was responsible for his death') and 'responsible' meaning 'accountable' ('A lieutenant is responsible to his senior officer for the welfare of his men').

If you say, 'I am responsible for the happiness of my family' are you saying, 'I cause my family to be happy, and if they are unhappy it is because I have failed to behave appropriately' or are you saying, 'I am accountable for my family's happiness, and if they are not happy the person I am accountable to (yourself? God?) will not be pleased with me'? In either case, is the statement 'I am responsible for my family's happiness' sensible?

No doubt when you were a child and being blamed for real and imagined misdemeanours you pondered the problem of cause. When an accident happens how do you decide who actually caused it?

Take the case of the RAF helicopter carrying senior people concerned with security in Northern Ireland, which, in foggy weather, flew into a mountain on the Mull of Kintyre. All those on board were killed. Who caused (was responsible) for this accident?

Was it:

the pilot, who was perhaps disoriented in the fog
the weatherman, who perhaps should have predicted the
density of the fog
the officer who had decided that the flight should take place
the government, whose policies made such a journey
necessary
the events in the history of Ireland and Britain which led to
the government's policies.

Once the line of causation gets to government policies it has
ceased to be linear (A leads to B, and B leads to C) and
has branched out into a network of causes. There is clearly no
one cause, but in the search for justice the blame will be laid
somewhere. Just where seems to depend on the position on the
network of causes of the person laying the blame. Those close
to the event often prefer to blame those higher up the hierarchy
and further from the event, while those further from the event
prefer to blame those close by.

If those not directly connected with the accident accept the
blame, the word 'responsibility' takes on more of a sense of
accountability. If there is a line of causation between the accident and government policies then the government is responsible because it has a duty to care for those who work for it and
it is responsible to (answerable to) the electors. One of the
corrupting effects of power is the refusal to accept the responsibility which goes along with the power.

A way of avoiding responsibility is to say that you are not
the last in the line of accountability. President Harry Truman
is seen as an honourable man because he said of himself and his
office, 'The buck stops here.'

Many people are not so brave and honourable. But what can
you do when you are the last in the hierarchy? Why, claim
that what has happened is 'God's will'. When fifteen hundred
pilgrims to Mecca died as a result of a bridge collapsing King
Fahd of Saudi Arabia explained, 'It was fate. Had they not died
there, they would have died elsewhere and at the predestined
moment.'[14]

Of course, if King Fahd had accepted that in the line of

responsibility the buck stopped with him, he would have had to pay compensation to the families of those who died. Being responsible can be expensive. So can being irresponsible. Charged with being responsible for other people and failing to be so can cost you your job.

Even more costly is failing to be responsible for yourself.

Here again 'responsible' means both 'cause' and 'account-ability'. You are deciding how well you have discharged your responsibility to yourself whenever you position yourself on your 'How I feel about myself' dimension. If one aspect of this dimension is, say, 'being a good parent' as against 'being a bad parent', being unpunctual in picking up your child from school is a failure of responsibility both to your child and to yourself. When you fail to live up to the standards you have set yourself you find yourself sliding down your 'How I feel about myself' dimension.

Being a harsh judge of yourself can lead you into error when deciding upon the limits of responsibility both as cause and as accountability.

You cannot be responsible for anything that happened before you were born. You didn't choose the set of genes you inherited, or the child-rearing practices of your parents and teachers, or the social, political, economic and religious conditions into which you were born.

When you judge your responsibility to others you need to remember that you can be responsible only for that which is within your competence to perform. Many parents torture themselves unnecessarily over this. As a parent with a new baby you do have control over much which affects your child, but not everything. You don't control the actions of the medical profession, you don't control the changing political and econ-omic conditions which affect your child, and even though your child inherited some of your genes you didn't choose which genes would be passed on.

Once your child ventures out of your home to nursery and then to school fewer and fewer of the influences on your child are under your control. You might be responsible for the choice of school your child goes to but not for what happens at that school. That is the responsibility of the school principal.

No matter what amount of control you have over other people and the conditions in which they live there is one important area where you can never have control and therefore responsibility.

You can never be responsible for the interpretations which other people create.

You can do everything possible to make your family happy, but if they want to interpret everything in terms of doom and disaster, that is their privilege. Each of us is responsible for the meanings we create and no one can take that responsibility from us. You act and are responsible for your actions, but you are not responsible for how other people interpret your actions. At work you can be all sweetness and light, but if your colleagues are convinced you're a devious sod you're stuck with their interpretation.

You are always responsible for your actions because what you do arises out of the interpretations you have made. You have chosen these interpretations rather than other interpretations. Saying, 'I had no choice' means 'I found all the other alternatives quite unacceptable'. Saying, 'I can't decide' means 'I have decided not to decide.'

You are not compelled to create any particular meanings though other people might try to compel you. They might tell you that God will punish you for your wicked thoughts or that to be accepted you must think as they do, but it is your choice whether you believe in a punitive God or whether you put being accepted by other people at the top of your priorities. Thought is private, so if you want to keep your interpretations secret, that is your privilege.

The essence of being responsible to and for yourself is to make your own interpretations and to acknowledge these interpretations. They are your own truth.

Your own truth is your identity. In a universe of constant change and uncertainty your identity is the only stability and certainty available to you – provided you meet your responsibility to yourself.

Vaclav Havel pondered these matters when he was in prison. In one of his letters to his wife Olga he wrote,

> If I know what I have done and why, and what I do and why, if I can really stand behind this and (in private perhaps) own up to it, I am thereby constantly relating to something stable, something I 'win' from my 'unstable' surroundings and thus I myself ultimately become 'relatively stable' – something graspable, something that possesses continuity and integrity. In short, I am 'someone', i.e., identical with himself. By standing today behind what I did yesterday, and standing here behind what I did elsewhere, I not only gain my identity, but through it, I find myself in space and time; if, on the contrary, I lose my identity, time and space must necessarily disintegrate around me as well. In this sense, therefore, responsibility establishes identity; it is only in the responsibility of human existence for what has been, is and will be that its identity dwells.[15]

Recognizing the prime importance of your responsibility to yourself to know your own truth and to know that you know what you know means also recognizing how little of the world and of your life you control.

It means recognizing the helplessness which is one of the inescapable conditions of human life.

The two extreme attitudes to responsibility – denying all responsibility and claiming total responsibility – are alike in that they are attempts to deny our helplessness.

Denying all responsibility is usually an attempt to avoid punishment and inconvenience, but it can also be an attempt to avoid the awareness of your helplessness when you have tried to act effectively and failed. On Black Wednesday, 16 September 1992, when the UK pound was forced out of the Exchange Rate Mechanism (ERM), the Prime Minister, John Major, and the Chancellor of the Exchequer, Norman Lamont, must have seen that their political power was as nothing against the power of the international money men (financiers, bankers, traders and speculators) who had decided that the pound was over-valued. Instead of acknowledging their helplessness, Major and Lamont denied that they had any responsibility for these events. They ignored the fact that they had presented themselves as most knowledgeable in money matters and as knowing what was best for the country when they took the UK into the ERM on terms unfavourable to the UK. Instead they presented the debacle as some kind of victory.

Those people who claim there are no limits to their responsibility are preferring to feel guilty than to feel helpless. To say that you feel guilty for some act or omission is to claim that you could have chosen to act differently. If you say, 'I am responsible for my family's happiness. If they're unhappy it's my fault' you are claiming:

1) that you control all the events which might affect your family's lives, such as the solvency of the firm which employs your son or the faithfulness of your daughter's husband

and

2) that you control how each member of your family interprets every event.

Claiming total responsibility is a devious way of getting power over other people. Your immense concern for the welfare of those for whom you claim responsibility shows how selfish and uncaring everyone else is, and, shamed, they hurry to do what you want. Knowing how guilty you feel at their failures, they strive to please you.

Total responsibility for others readily transforms itself into martyrdom, which is the bid for power often chosen by those who have no claim on political and economic power (hence its popularity amongst mothers and wives).[16]

There could be situations where you might decide to deny all responsibility or claim total responsibility while at the same time acknowledging to yourself an appropriate degree of responsibility. However, those people who frequently deny all responsibility or claim total responsibility are more likely to be

lying to themselves even more keenly than they are lying to others.

Denying all responsibility or claiming total responsibility will not make you loved and trusted by other people. Worse, both practices prevent you from discharging your prime responsibility, that of your responsibility to yourself, your own truth.

If you cannot be responsible for yourself, how can you be responsible for anyone else?

CHAPTER 14

You and Communication

THE SCIENTISTS who study how our species came into being say that our ancestors of many millions of years ago communicated with one another using no more than a few grunts, squeals and gestures. Then for some reason (scientists can't agree what) some of our ancestors (scientists can't agree which) began to think and talk (scientists can't agree whether talking led to thinking or vice versa). Our early ancestors had spent millions of years plodding around doing much the same things generation after generation and then suddenly a few thousand years ago (scientists can't agree how many) people began telling stories and telling lies, writing plays and fraudulent cheques, singing love songs and suing for divorce, signing peace treaties and buying arms, seeking truth by reading God's word and turning on the telly. Oceans and ice floes, deserts and mountains had kept our ancestors in their separate groups with their separate languages but now Rupert Murdoch, Ted Turner and Bill Gates have brought us all together. We can communicate superbly.

Or can we?

What is communication but a mutual misunderstanding? Our problem is that our basic structure as a human being ensures that we will always misunderstand one another.

When a computer manufacturer sets out to build computers which can communicate with certain other computers he makes sure that his computers have the same basic software as the other computers. Unfortunately, our Master Designer (if there was one – perhaps we just evolved) failed to provide each of us with compatible software. We've all, more or less, got the same basic hardware, but we've each got our own little unique piece of software. To add to our problems, when we try to communicate we have to use a very faulty medium called language.

Many of the mistakes we make in understanding ourselves and other people come from faults inherent in language. Some of these faults are inherent in all the languages that have ever been spoken and some are peculiar to particular languages.

One of the problems with English and the other Indo-European languages has to do with the way these languages prefer nouns to verbs. (The Hopi language, so I am told, doesn't have this problem, but not many people speak Hopi.)

Nouns, as I'm sure you know, are naming words and verbs are doing words. For a group of words to be a sentence it has to have a verb. 'The cat sat on the mat' is a sentence. 'The cat the mat' is not. Important though verbs are, English prefers nouns. Verbs are turned into nouns, which would be fine, except that we often think that if we have a noun (a name) there must be something existing to which the noun refers.

For instance, I see you coughing and sneezing (verbs) and I say, 'I see you have a cold.' I have turned what you are doing into a thing, a cold. I now say, 'Don't give me your cold', as if you could hand me a cold in the way you could hand me a cup of tea. Yet there is no such thing as 'a cold'. When certain viruses and bacteria are present in your body you behave in a particular way and when they aren't you don't.

This process of turning verbs into nouns has a name – reification, making into a thing. Reification bedevils psychiatry and psychology and the way we talk about what we do.

You might say to your doctor, 'I've got no reason to feel miserable but I do. I can't eat or sleep. I feel very anxious and I keep worrying about all the things I've done wrong.'

You're describing what you're doing. Your doctor wants to give what you're doing a name (a diagnosis) so he says, 'You have endogenous depression.'

You had been wondering why you were feeling miserable, anxious and guilty but now you're being told that the situation isn't what you thought. You thought you were *doing* something and now you're told you *have* something. If it's something you have in the way you have an overcoat why don't you give your depression away? Your doctor gives you some pills which, he says, 'Will get rid of your depression.' When you don't get any better you feel guilty because you must be still hanging on to this thing called depression.

You do have a problem here, but it's one created by language.

Psychologists have been just as idiotic as psychiatrists in turning what we do into non-existent things which we are supposed to 'have'. They turned behaving intelligently into 'intelligence' and spent years researching how to measure this mythical thing. More recently they have created a thing called self-esteem. Have you got 'low self-esteem'? If so, you should swap it for 'high self-esteem'. If you haven't got much self-esteem why don't you pop into the self-esteem shop and buy some more?

Clumsy though the phrase '"How I feel about myself" dimension' is, I use it to help you remember that this is something you *do*. It's not something you have. Something you do can become a habit (that is, doing something over and over again and not thinking about what you are doing), but while some habits are hard to break because they provide certain rewards, all habits can be changed. You just do something else.

If you want to change you need to inspect the language you use. Be aware of when you are thinking you have (or don't have) something when in fact what you should be thinking about is something you *do*.

Reification is an example of using the wrong metaphor. You can make this mistake in whatever language you speak because all languages are metaphorical. The word metaphor, used of words, is itself a metaphor. It means, literally, a "carrying over". In modern Greek it still carries its literal as well as figurative meaning. The adjective *metaphoroikos* refers to any means of physical transport. *Metaphoréas*, 'a carrier', may refer to the national airline or to a railway porter . . . Metaphors are carriers. Human beings are carriers of metaphors.'[17]

To talk about anything, to give it a meaning, we have to say what it is like, and what we say it is like (the metaphor) determines what we can say about it.

This problem is inherent in language because of the way our

meaning structure works. You encounter a new situation. The only way you can make sense of it is in terms of your past experience. So you create a metaphor.

Nigel Lewis in his book *The Tower of Babel* said that when the ancient Norwegians saw the Atlantic they called it *blamyra*, the blue moor. When his two-year-old son first saw the sea he cried, 'Juice!'[18] Sally Laird, reviewing Lewis's book, said that her two-year-old called the sea 'the big bath'.[19] Each of these metaphors captures an aspect of the sea, but to use any of these metaphors as an accurate representation of the sea would lead to disaster. Our bodies don't respond well to prolonged bathing in the sea, nor to drinking it, while walking on water is a rare skill.

Metaphors capture only certain aspects of the phenomena they refer to and the content of the metaphor determines what can be said about the phenomena.

For instance, if certain behaviour is described by the metaphor 'illness' then everything that can be said about that behaviour has to be in terms of illness – physical cause, diagnosis, treatment, management, cure. The metaphor does not allow for other concepts like 'learning' and 'choice'.

Throughout this book I have been using the metaphor of a dimension or straight line with something moving up and down that line in order to talk about certain profound feelings which we all experience. I am trying to clarify the issues involved so I use a very simple metaphor.

However, I would be very stupid if I thought that such a metaphor could encapsulate the vastness and complexities of those feelings. All the great literature of the world, dealing as it does with people's feelings in relation to themselves, cannot achieve this. Moreover, reflecting on feelings is a different experience from feeling those feelings. It can be a useful exercise to draw a straight line and each day mark on it how well or badly you are thinking of yourself. You might notice how you plunge down the dimension after a visit from your mother and fly up the dimension when your boss praises your work, and such an observation might suggest certain changes which would be to your advantage. However, to believe that inside you is a real thing called self-esteem which goes up and down like mercury in a thermometer is ludicrous.

Metaphors which we acquire very early in life and which we constantly use don't appear to us as being metaphors and instead seem to be absolute reality. This effect is much strengthened when the adults around us insist that these metaphors are not metaphors but absolute reality. As a result we can be unaware of what falls outside the scope of the metaphor and how the metaphor limits what we can say.

Suppose you're born into a family which has very strict fundamentalist religious or political beliefs. You are immediately presented with a metaphor for describing and explaining everything in the world. The metaphor is that of the battle between the forces of good and evil, which might be equated with God and the Devil or Communism and Capitalism. The metaphor is applied to everybody and everything. There is good behaviour and bad behaviour, good people and bad people.

You learn to assess yourself and other people according to this metaphor. If everyone within your family and immediate environment uses this metaphor you find while you're a child that life is simple and straightforward, and pleasant if you become an expert in being good.

However, this metaphor does not acknowledge the complexities of human behaviour and consequently you do not learn the skills necessary to assess those people whose behaviour is a mixture of good and bad (all of us) nor of identifying those people who do not assess themselves in terms of the good/bad metaphor.

You grow up and go out into the world. You might think of yourself as being tremendously intelligent and well-educated, but as long as the good/bad metaphor remains central to your meaning structure and unrecognized as a metaphor you remain naive in your assessment of others. You tend to take people at face value and fail to see their complexity and their capacity for doing good for bad reasons and doing bad for good reasons. Meet someone who does not operate on a good/bad dimension and you are lost.

All the metaphors we use to describe and explain our life take the form of a story. The good/bad metaphor is the story of good triumphing over evil. This story has a multitude of versions and not all these versions are compatible. The most popular version is 'If I am good I shall be rewarded', and this becomes the basis of many people's life stories.

Another popular version is that of the tragic hero (or heroine). You in your naive state can be God's gift to the person who is set upon a tragic path, who sees themselves as a suffering, lone figure on a mountain top silhouetted against the sky. On such a path all opportunities for mere happiness are spurned. The hero is traduced, humiliated and injured by those wicked, uncaring people who, at the end of the story, will realize his superhuman virtue and, shamed and guilty, beg his forgiveness. But it will be too late. The hero is with them no more.

The enactment of such a story can take a lifetime and the hero, whose suffering can take the form of an undiagnosable illness, a depression resistant to all forms of treatment, or an unrecognized (and unrecognizable) artistic talent, needs someone who, committed to being and doing good, will never cast a critical eye upon the enactment of the story nor see it as a story but will work unceasingly to alleviate the hero's sufferings just as constantly as the hero will create new forms of suffering. Friends might wonder why the couple stay together since they give one another so little joy, and they might comment on how poorly the two seem to communicate. Perceptive friends will see that the couple live their lives in terms of two very different metaphors. Each is trying to force life to conform to their cherished metaphor, yet for life actually to conform to one of the metaphors means that the other has to fail. Alas, as ever, life will go its own merry way.

All versions of the goodness triumphing over evil story, be they about doing good works or having intrinsic virtue, are attempts to deny death. To deny death, death has first to be acknowledged. Some people in childhood are so terrified by the abandonment and utter aloneness which death brings that they turn away from it and refuse to acknowledge it. Instead they construct a metaphor for life where death has no part. Life, they say, is about playing 'Let's pretend'. They make up stories and enact them always with themselves as a chief protagonist. Other people can have walk-on parts. All these stories are versions of the person's life story which is 'If I am entertaining, dramatic, enticing and charming, people will notice me.' The hidden part of the metaphor is 'and I won't die'.

Along comes naive you seeing life as real and earnest. You might be repulsed by the frivolity of this person, or you might become entranced and soon find yourself being an actor in the play. However, you don't know it's a play. You think it's real. You become confused by the sudden changes of plot, the paucity or the unreliability of the explanations you are given. If you're lucky you soon recognize that what you're seeing is the 'Let's pretend' metaphor where concepts of right and wrong are rarely used and then only for their dramatic possibilities. It dawns on you that people who use the 'Let's pretend' metaphor should be enjoyed but never taken seriously or made a central part of your life. If you're unlucky your disillusionment is accompanied by the realization that there are children requiring your support or a police officer requiring your arrest.

We come together as lovers or friends whenever we interpret the other person as having characteristics which we associate with forms of happiness and satisfaction we encountered in childhood and as sharing the metaphor whereby we live our life. Any man who in some way reminds me of my father and who makes me laugh brings a twinkle to my eye. My friends share my metaphor that life is interesting and should be enjoyed. Being right in our judgements about our friends is immensely pleasurable, being wrong can be disastrous.

Often we misinterpret what is happening because we fail to observe closely what is actually happening. We then use a wrong metaphor which leads us further astray. This happens constantly when we talk about communication.

Whenever we talk about any aspect of communication we use a metaphor which does not reflect what actually happens. When we don't realize this we can become very puzzled over our frequent failures in communication.

Suppose that on a cold day you come to visit me. I say to you, 'Give me your coat.' You hand me your coat and I hang

when we first met Life was A FeAst!
he was Great fUn — charminG
spontaneous, GEnerous and WilD.
Since leaving me with the
tWins and several debts it's
rapidly beCoMe an episode
in a VERY bad Soap OpERA.
MY adviCE is. don'T MiX yoUr
METAPHORS !

it up. Once you're seated I say to you, 'Give me your news.'

Am I expecting you to hand me a little packet labelled 'My News'? No. I expect you to start talking, communicating with me. I hear your words. Is what I'm asking for some *thing* which is contained in your words? Do you send this thing down the pipeline of your words and I receive it at my end of your pipeline?

If this were the case I would get from you exactly what you intended to give me, just as the coat I received from you is the same one as you handed to me. In such a transaction there can be no mistakes. What I hear and absorb is exactly what you told me. Or is it?

Of course not. What I hear and absorb is not what you tell me. What I get is what I create. I don't get your news. I get my interpretation of your news.

Moreover, when I ask you for your news you might think that I want to hear about certain events in your life. But that isn't what you give me. What you give me is your interpretation of these events.

Every act of communication follows this pattern:

- An event occurs
- Person A interprets that event in terms of Person A's past experience.
- Person A passes this interpretation to Person B.
- Person B interprets Person A's interpretation in terms of Person B's past experience.

The way we talk about communication does not reflect how every act of communication contains at least two different interpretations. Instead we use a metaphor which implies that what is communicated travels inside something from one person to another or is contained inside something and can be discovered. We say,

'I don't get what you mean.'
'He poured out all his feelings.'
'That book is full of good advice.'
'You haven't put any new concepts in your report.'
'He got all his ideas from his father.'

The linguist Michael Reddy calls this the *conduit metaphor*.[20] If this metaphor actually reflected what we do our communications would never fail. Instead, not only do our communications often fail but we can be oblivious to the tricks that are played on us.

Every day most of us watch or listen to what we call 'the news'. Yet there is no such thing as 'the news'. What we see and hear are the interpretations of certain events made by certain people (usually men) in power in the media. These are the

people who decide policy or carry out policy. Their interpretations are made for reasons which might relate to truth and
public interest but which more likely relate to their own interests. They want us to keep watching and listening so that they
will keep their jobs and their power. When we're watching
television, listening to the radio or reading a newspaper we
should ask, 'Why am I being told this?'

We should ask the same question whenever we listen to or
read some account which purports to be history. There is no
one True History but as many histories as there are people to
tell the story. History is written from a particular point of view
and for a particular purpose, a purpose not necessarily for the
benefit of the history's audience. A country's official history is
history as told by the victors. The vanquished tell a different
tale.

The history of anthropology is not just the history of important finds but also the history of anthropologists trying to fit
their findings and their theories into a story which would further
the anthropologist's own ends. Some of these ends are noble
and some are not. Anthropologists do, however, agree that
somewhere in our past our early ancestors developed thought
and language.

When our ancestors discovered how to think and talk they
also made another important discovery. They could reflect upon
their own thinking and talking.

By such reflection it is possible for you to become aware of
your own meaning structure and to know what you know. This
process isn't easy because you can study your meaning structure
only in your meaning structure's own terms. Hence it is important to make sure that your terms are wide-ranging and flexible.

If you define your self-reflection in terms of rooting out your
evil thoughts and replacing them with good ones, or of discovering a neurosis to be analysed or an Inner Child to be
cosseted, or of proving once and for all that your parents are
to blame for all your misery, these terms, or metaphors, will
determine what you will find. On the other hand, if you choose
the metaphor of going on a journey, a metaphor used by people
down the ages for the gaining of wisdom, and if you realize

that what is valuable is not the distant (and non-existent) goal but what you find along the way, you are using a metaphor which makes the discovery of your own truth possible. If you search for The Final Truth you will be disappointed, but if you search for your truth and the truths which other people have found to be important you will find that every step of the journey uncovers another prize.

Such a journey is sometimes scary, but what can be even more scary is to set out to explore another person's meaning structure.

I saw this when as part of my work I talked to couples where one partner was depressed or in some other kind of distress. Having been together a long time each would claim to know the other well. I would start an exploration of the meaning structure of each person using those simple but powerful questions, 'How do you feel about that?' and 'Why is that important to you?' At some point in the conversation the person I was questioning would say something and the partner, in total surprise, would burst out with, 'I never knew you felt like that!' Not all these couples stayed together. How could they when they had discovered they were living with a stranger.

We often use language like we often use sex, as a way of avoiding communication. Realizing that someone familiar inhabits a different world from us makes us aware of our own essential aloneness. Yet until we actually want to communicate and so become prepared to learn how to communicate we shall continue to inflict suffering on one another.

Henry Beston, writing about how little we understand animals, said,

> Remote from universal nature, and living by complicated artifice, man in civilization surveys the creature through the glass of his knowledge and sees thereby a feather magnified and the whole image in distortion. We patronize them for their incompleteness, for their tragic fate of having taken form so far below ourselves. And therein we err, and greatly err. For the animal shall not be measured by man. In a world older and more complete than ours they move more finished and complete, gifted with extensions of

senses we have lost or never attained, living by voices we shall never hear. They are not brethren, they are not underlings; they are other nations, caught with ourselves in the net of life and time, fellow prisoners of the splendour and travail of the earth.[21]

Alas, just as we misinterpret animals so we misinterpret other people. We think that our way of seeing things is the only right way to see things and we forget that we are all 'fellow prisoners of the splendour and travail of the earth'.

However, we are free to change.

CHAPTER 15

You and the World

WE TALK of being on the planet Earth but being in the world. 'In' certainly accords with our direct experience of the land beneath our feet, the sky overhead and the meeting of the land (or sea) and sky at the horizon. However, when we talk about 'the world' we mean more than the container formed by the earth and sky. We mean all those people, animals, things and places that are on the planet Earth. We see ourselves as being in this world and yet as individuals in contrast to it. Although the world exists in space and time separate from us, how we interpret the world is directly linked with how we interpret ourselves.

We might all agree that the world consists of land, sky, mountains, rivers, oceans, trees, plants, animals, planes, boats, buildings, people and all the objects they possess. Many of us would say that the world also includes ghosts and spirits and forces unknown to science, such as the forces of good and evil or karma or those influences from the planets which (perhaps) direct our lives. For some people such spirits and forces are simply ideas which they use to explain events. They no more see these ghostly beings and forces than I see the force of gravity. For others the spirits and forces are as real as trees and people. The world they look upon is very different from the one I see.

What we actually see in the world depends on what we've learned to see. As the old saying ought to go, 'If I hadn't have believed it I wouldn't have seen it.'

An Indian professor of psychology once took me boating

at the place where the brown waters of the Ganges meet the blue-green waters of the Jumna. This is a very holy place for the Hindus and, as is their wont in holy places, many of them bathe there. The professor explained to me that the waters of the Ganges are always pure. As I sat in the boat facing him I could see just beyond his shoulder a part of some large thing, wrapped in cloth and bobbing in the water. I realized that I certainly didn't see the Ganges in the way that he did.

This is to be expected because I didn't grow up in India. However I did grow up in Australia and I see the Australian bush differently from how I see its equivalent anywhere else in the world. Although I know that the bush provides few conditions which are supportive to human life, I experience the bush as being friendly, accepting of me and safe – all human qualities.

Seeing the natural world and inanimate objects as possessing human attributes is another example of how we give meaning to a new situation by interpreting it in terms of our past experience. We are born looking for faces to whom we can relate. The conclusions we draw from these early experiences become the interpretations we use to understand everything we encounter, human or otherwise. As small children we see our toys and pets and the other animals we encounter as being human. If the people around us prove to be too difficult to be close to we might impose better than human qualities on to animals or certain prized possessions. For many men their car or motor bike or computer has far better than human qualities.

On the other hand, if the majority of the conclusions you drew from your early experience were that people were kind and caring, that you were loved and wanted and that your home was where you belonged you would have interpreted your experiences of the world in those terms. You would have had the comfortable security of knowing that this is where you belong and here is not only the best place in the universe but it is the centre of the universe. (The Chinese have always seen China as the centre of the universe whereas my friend Ron knows that New York is.)

I didn't have that experience. The bush seemed friendly to

me because that was where I escaped to when life with my mother became too painful. Mother didn't follow me into the bush or to the beach so I was able to preserve the delight these places gave me. I was luckier than those people who lose their delight in the entire world.

I was reminded of just how easily this can happen when a few months ago I made a visit to Bristol.

Over the years I had lived in England I had visited Bristol on many occasions and each time I had enjoyed myself. Everything I had done in Bristol – visiting friends, teaching, talking on radio, publicizing my books – had turned out well. I saw Bristol as being a delightful, interesting city and I was always pleased to return there. However, a recent visit was different. I took part in a television production. Such events can be a very enjoyable experience but sometimes they aren't. This experience was the worst I had ever had. I felt used and deceived. Home again, I looked in my diary to see what the week had in store. There was the entry, four days ahead, showing that I would be going again to Bristol. My whole being revolted at the thought. I wanted never to set foot in that place ever again.

Bristol had done nothing to harm me. It was the same pleasant place. What had happened was that all those black, miserable, frustrated and despairing feelings that had risen inside me during and after my last experiences there had overflowed and besmirched my idea of Bristol.

Fortunately I recognized what had happened. Instead of inventing reasons why I couldn't go to Bristol or of going and having an unhappy time, I made a conscious effort to withdraw my bad feelings from Bristol and put them where they belonged, on those who had used me and other people as objects of little importance in order to further their own ends.

Being treated as an object always has the effect of pushing you down your 'How I feel about myself' dimension. If there is no one else around who treats you as a valued person you can slide to the bottom and those black, miserable, frustrated and despairing feelings come welling up and spilling out, contaminating everything around you.

Those feelings can contaminate every aspect of what you call 'me'. You can come to hate your appearance, even your own name. When I was about eight I found among some papers in a drawer photographs of my mother as a bride. She was very beautiful. When Mother saw me looking at them and giggling as children do at pictures of their parents in their younger days she, angry and embarrassed, took them from me and ripped them to pieces. Throughout her life Mother always said that she hated her name, Ella Barbara. Friends she had known for decades always called her Mrs Conn.

Those same black feelings can contaminate every aspect of what you call 'world'.

Babies find the world delightful. They are curious about the world just for the pleasure of discovering and knowing. They enjoy the world in the present, the here and now. Within your meaning structure somewhere is a memory of experiences of joy, delight and pleasure around you and through you in the here and now.

However, that memory is overlaid with other memories of failing, being inadequate or wicked, memories of being criticized, punished, humiliated, rejected, abandoned, memories of dark, miserable, frustrated and despairing feelings welling up, suffusing you, spilling out, covering and soaking into your world, turning it into a cold, grey, empty, alien prison. Thus you learned to hate yourself and to hate the world.

How can you survive in such a place? Life is unbearable if you have no hope of anything better. You feel that nothing better could happen in your present world. So you tell yourself that something better lies beyond this world. There is Heaven, or Paradise, or Nirvana, or the world in another time which will be happier for you. Or you tell yourself that this world is merely one of appearances and behind it lies a Reality finer, more beautiful, more trustworthy than this world could ever be.

With such beliefs you might find a certain security, but at a terrible price. From now on you have to live your life not in the present, as you did as a small child, but in terms of the far future you have imagined. Now you have to tailor your actions to fit the demands of this other, better world. The existence of this other world tells you that what you're living now isn't real life. Real life lies in the future.

To gain entry to such a real life you have to meet the standards set by this future realm of being. Such standards pertain to everything you do. In a group of mature university students one woman told us how, even though she was her family's breadwinner and her partner a happy househusband, when she arrived home from work each evening she couldn't put her feet up and read the paper while he got dinner. She had to do the domestic chores.

'What would my mother think of me if I didn't!' she said, showing how she had accepted her mother's belief that life should be lived in terms of the future. After all, Satan finds mischief for idle hands to do.

Some people manage to preserve some small part of their world as untarnished. They might still be able to experience their garden or their pets or music in immediate delight as they did when they were young. For other people their world in its entirety is dark and evil. In a public debate over whether the media presented too much bad news and not enough good, one advocate for more good news said that the plethora of bad news spewed out by the media formed an evil whirlpool. All of us were on the edge of the whirlpool and increasingly in danger of being sucked down into it.

How terrible it must be to believe that you live in such a world! Even worse, not to understand that the world looks like that to you because that's how you've interpreted it. Not to know that the whirlpool is your metaphor, not a reality.

The world simply is. It is neither good nor bad. 'Good' and 'bad' are our ideas. The world, like everything else that exists, is constantly changing. In the course of such change a volcano might erupt. If you're some distance away the volcano might look magnificent. If you're up close it might look dangerous. But the volcano is neither magnificent nor dangerous. The magnificent and dangerous volcano is part of your meaning structure.

Volcanoes do not harbour intentions to charm or harm you. People harbour intentions and act on them, and so much of

WHen I've TOLD soCiaL WORKERS
THe STorY OF MY life THEY ve SUGGested
its Been MORE LiKe A GREEK TragEDY.
But I Look At it **like this** - i can Still Remember every dirty joke
i've ever heard - AND I Laugh all The TIME with my maTES. of every
experience of every kind yes I said yes I will
Yes

human activity cannot be viewed and encountered with joy and delight. But to reject the whole world because some people behave badly is foolishness indeed.

Belief in some other better world is necessary for those people who want to believe that there is some over-arching Grand Design which ensures that the wicked are punished and the good rewarded. Evidence of such an outcome is sadly lacking in this particular world, so believers in a Just World have to hope there is another world where justice reigns supreme.

Brought up to believe that there is a place for everything and everything must be in its place, many people find it impossible to accept the ambiguity that is inherent in our existence. They want to see their life and their world as being as controlled and organized as a game of chess. They do not want to see that the world cannot be so neat because everything that happens has good outcomes and bad outcomes and that every interpretation we make has good implications and bad implications.

It is the ambiguity of our lives and the world which makes living a surprise and a delight. This is why babies love playing 'Peek a Boo' and why we all prefer stories where the ending is not obvious at the beginning. (Murder mysteries are popular because they combine ambiguity and surprise with, ultimately, a place for everything and everything in its place. In real life murder and its aftermath are rarely so neat.)

It is only because life is ambiguous and uncertain that we can hope. An unambiguous and certain world would be a world where there was no place for hope, a hopeless world.

If you refuse to accept the ambiguity of your life and the world and instead try to force your life and the world to be unambiguous, certain and ordered, you become frustrated, angry and despairing.

If you reject the world because you see it as evil and alien, you create for yourself an aloneness far worse than that of ordinary human aloneness because you live in fear of this evil, alien world.

If you reject yourself for being bad and unacceptable you live your life not in the present but in the past and the future, feeling guilty about the past and fearful of what the future must bring.

If you reject the world you cannot live in the present, yet it is only in the present that you can know joy, delight, happiness and contentment.

The world as you know it is inside you. So is time.

CHAPTER 16

You and Time

WE LIVE in the world and we live in time. We measure time so that everyone can agree what time it is. Yet each of us has our own individual experience of time.

How do you picture yourself and time?

This is a question I asked a number of people when I was researching for my book *Time on Our Side*. In asking this question I discovered that my picture of time and me had changed over the years. I used to see time as a wind blowing past me but now it is a moving walkway.

The picture I see now is that time is like one of those moving walkways found in large airports. However, my time walkway is infinitely long and moves from the past into the future. When as a tiny child I woke to self-awareness I discovered myself on this walkway. I walked along the walkway and for my first three decades time and I kept pace with one another but then, though my pace remained the same, the walkway got faster and faster. Now the past lengthens behind me far beyond the point where I joined the walkway but ahead the walkway disappears into a mist which is coming closer and closer.

I can see a relationship between this image and how I feel about my life right now. For instance, I recently read in my favourite paper, the *Guardian*, that Rupert Murdoch was reported to have said that in ten or twenty years' time there would be only three national newspapers, the *Sun*, *The Times* and the *Daily Mail*. Ten years ago such a remark would have enraged me, but now my immediate thought was, 'I won't be here to see that.'

The people I asked to draw a picture of their relationship to time were people I knew well. I found that I could easily see a relationship between their picture and their lives.

My friend John, a very successful businessman, drew a series of mountain ranges and above them a line of clocks disappearing off into the distance. He drew himself running up the side of the first mountain and, in keeping with the confidence he has in his ability to surmount difficulties, his figure is larger than the mountains.

During a summer vacation David at fourteen drew an hourglass at the centre of his picture. From bottom left to top right time was traversed by yellow suns and yellow cloud representing summer vacations. To the top left and bottom right were two heavy, black august buildings representing school. Beyond each of these were the promises of the future, a mortar board and a diploma, each emitting rays of golden light. David explained that he was caught in the school cycle. 'This vacation is too short and I'm not looking forward to another year of high school.'

David's picture presents time both as a circle and as a line into the future. Those of us who grew up in industrialized countries are used to time being presented in a linear fashion along with the idea of progress — a way of interpreting life which became popular only during the Industrial Revolution. Before then life was not seen in terms of progress except in so far as the good could see themselves progressing to heaven and the wicked to hell. Ordinary life was dominated by the recurring round of the seasons. In societies where each generation lived a life much the same as all the successive generations time was circular. The Balinese saw a grandson as being the reincarnation of his dead grandfather.

Our experience of time is very curious. When we're enjoying ourselves time goes quickly. When we're bored it drags. As we get older time goes faster and faster. We talk about space and time as if they are equal attributes of our world, yet we can go back and forth in space but not in time. We cannot revisit our yesterdays.

If we turn to physicists to find out what time *really* is we get confusing answers. In what physicists call their classical theories time as a one-way path disappears and in space-time the events of the universe are laid out. The theories work equally well with time going forwards or backwards. However, in the Second Law of Thermodynamics, which is about how things wear out, time accords with our experience. Time goes only one way. Heat always flows from the hot water bottle to the cold sheets, not from the sheets making them colder and the water bottle hotter.

For many years philosophers argued about the nature of time but now it is seen that 'Our sense of time is neither a necessary condition of our experience, as Kant thought, nor a simple sensation, as Mach believed, but an intellectual construction.'[22]

What we know as time is an interpretation just like everything else we experience.

Part of our experience of time is our experience of getting older.

Getting older is not an experience which most people face with equanimity. When we're children most of us look forward to being grown up because we see adults as being free of constraints and able to make their own decisions. However, by the time we are in our teens we see people in their late twenties as being past their best and those over thirty as being old and finished.

Many people in their twenties, I have found, see thirty as the peak of life and after that is downhill all the way.

Some people set themselves goals such as making a million or being at the top of their profession by their thirtieth birthday. If they succeed they are left wondering what to do with the rest of their lives, and if they don't succeed they fall into despair.

Having discovered that there is life after thirty many people decide that forty is the turning point. Being over forty means that you're old and useless. Unfortunately this has now become business management gospel. The directors of the Midland Bank decided to dispose of most of their employees over fifty on the grounds that their customers wanted to see young, dynamic staff.[24] They didn't ask my opinion. I prefer to see bank staff

"*Good heavens, Dorian – how dreadful!*" 23

who know what they are doing irrespective of what age they are.

Being in your forties does bring some extraordinary experiences. There is the sense of incredulity that so many years have gone by, a feeling which increases with passing time. The Sixties generation who are now in their forties cannot believe that their decade, the most important decade in the history of the human race, is itself history. Yet in a twinkling of an eye they will be like the little old men and women around us now who did something special back in the ancient time of the Forties, something to do with a war.

Of course by the time we're in our forties we have seen the adults who in our childhood were strong and vigorous grow frail and old. The sight of old age, like the sight of death, reminds us of ourselves and we grow frightened.

Then in our fifties we look in the mirror and see, not ourselves, but our mother or father. Who can this old person be when you're still the person you've always been?

Now you discover a strange phenomenon. By your late fifties or early sixties you have become invisible to people younger than you. Salespersons and waiters are oblivious of your custom, and you learn to dodge the pedestrians who look at you as they come towards you but don't see you. Men who are rich and powerful are still visible in terms of their riches and power but, unless women become outrageously noticeable like Joan Collins or Barbara Cartland, they become unseen ghosts. Some of us find this peaceful and useful (no longer harassed by men and able to observe without being observed) but for others invisibility destroys their self-confidence. Many older women in public wear a sweet, placating smile, grateful that their existence is being tolerated.

Even if you in your seventies, eighties and nineties are strong, vigorous and leading a full life you will still be patronized by those younger than you. If you become frail and ill you will be deemed to be as foolish and incapable as a young child but far less interesting. The fact that you wish to be treated with respect and dignity as a person in your own right will be of no interest to those who claim to care for you.

With such a prospect it's not surprising that when we're young we fear getting old, especially when we fail to realize that every age, like everything else in life, has advantages and disadvantages and that we should make the most of the advantages and minimize the disadvantages. What we need to do is to become aware of our disadvantageous attitudes and practices and change them.

The same applies to other events which are regarded as the inevitable losses involved in getting older.

There is the waning of sexual potency which many men fear and the waning of sexual attractiveness which many women fear. Whether a man or a woman loses sexual potency depends on circumstances, not on some physical inevitability. Boredom and loss of confidence destroy desire and performance, but most destructive of all are the unreal expectations which most people place on sex.

As small children we are interested in everything and are infinitely talented. However, our education destroys our

25

curiosity and we are taught that we are not the artists, musicians, writers, singers, scientists and inventors we had once thought.

How then can we express that strong urge to live and experience and create? By calling our essence of life 'sexuality'. Everything that we want to experience and express, everything that might make our life worth living we have to express through the medium of sex, a medium which is only one small part of our potentiality.

We become obsessed by sex and disappointed and betrayed by sex.

So much of our obsession with sex focuses on sexual attractiveness. We behave as if the standards of beauty are immutable laws of the universe although the evidence is all around us that beauty is in one place only, the eye of the beholder. At present in our society we learn to see beauty as solely an attribute of the young. We become oblivious to all other kinds of beauty. We do not need, as Japanese does, the word *shibui*, the beauty of ageing.

The progress of medical science often shows not a disinterested pursuit of knowledge and a desire to alleviate suffering but a financial interest in those people deemed to be important. The chief beneficiaries of the advances in heart surgery are white, middle-aged, middle class men. There are no equivalent advances in medical knowledge and practice in the areas of the female menstrual cycle and menopause and the care of the elderly. Yet all this could change with a change of opinion.

Medical science cannot abolish death, but if we lifted our taboo on talking about death we could find ways of helping one another to face the loss of loved ones and our own death.

Thus all the inevitable difficulties we encounter with increasing age are matters which we could change simply by changing our interpretations and thus our actions. Why haven't we done this? Why is our fear of growing old so unnecessarily great?

There are two reasons for this. One arises from the way children are and have always been treated and the other from our ignorance of what in life is inevitable.

Even today many of the world's people live close to the land and at the mercy of the climate. This is how we all once lived. In those conditions when famine came upon a tribe decisions had to be made as to who in the tribe should live. If the tribe was to continue those adults who had learned all the skills necessary for survival and who could repopulate the tribe needed to survive. Children could not ensure the survival of the tribe and so they were left to die. Today in famine areas in Somalia, Ethiopia and the Sudan children are sent to the feeding centres by their families but are forbidden to eat. Instead they have to bring the food back to give to the adults.[26]

Survival of the tribe meant that children should be seen as objects to be used and discarded as the needs of the tribe dictated. Unfortunately, as social conditions evolved and physical survival became less marginal, this attitude to children did not change. The history of the human race is the history of the tragedy of children used and abused by adults.

We live in a society which hates children. There are certain adults who love and respect certain children, but children, all children, are not valued and respected as individuals in their own right. If we valued children we would organize our society so that no child lived in poverty and was denied a good education.

Throughout history those children who survived their treatment learned to fear and hate adults. Most children dealt with the pain they suffered by becoming indifferent to it, and thus became indifferent to the suffering of other people. As adults they were able to do to children what had been done to them. To such indifference they could add as they got old their envy of the young for having the attributes which they had lost.

In rigid societies where the old held absolute power the young were required to honour the old. Such societies are often held up as examples of how we ought to live, with the old getting the honour and respect they claim to deserve. However, when such societies begin to crumble, as has happened in West Africa, among Muslim communities in the UK and in parts of present day China, the young reveal the hatred they have for the old. They treat the old no better than do the young in societies where the old have little power.

We all learn in childhood to fear and hate the old. Even if our parents unfailingly treat us with respect we encounter at school and elsewhere adults who do not. In adult life, even if we unfailingly treat the young with respect, we still find ourselves seen by the young as objects of their derision, envy and spite. No wonder we all fear growing old!

Yet we could change all this. We could bring up our children with respect and understanding.

There is another reason why we fear growing old.

If we understood ourselves and the world we live in we would know that everything is connected to everything else and that all acts have consequences. Regrettably, most of us live in our teens, twenties and thirties as if our actions have no consequences at all or only very limited consequences. In our forties we usually start to get an inkling that our actions in the past do have consequences. Our skies darken with the wings of vultures coming home to roost.

Such vultures come in all shapes and sizes, but here are some of the most common.

If you believe that you live in a Just World where goodness is rewarded and badness punished and that you have been good and thus deserve rewards, you become bitter and resentful when the rewards you expect do not materialize. Your bitterness and resentment alienate all who know you.

If you believe that you live in a Just World where goodness is rewarded and badness punished and that although you have tried to be good you are not good enough, when disaster strikes you, you become depressed.

If you believe that someone has injured you and that you must be revenged no matter what the cost, the cost is a life of misery.

If you believe that nothing is of any importance other than sex and sport, or your home and family, or your work, or your ambition, your life will gradually become emptier and lonelier until all you have is emptiness and loneliness.

If you believe that you must get everything for yourself and do whatever suits you, irrespective of anyone else's needs and wishes, you will find yourself excluded from other people's lives. Why should they bother about you when you never bothered about them?

If you seek to control people by making them frightened of you, no matter how kind you are to them at other times, they will fear you, hate you, not love you, and shut you out of their lives.

If you seek to control people by making them feel guilty they will come to hate you because they feel helpless, or they will deride and ignore you.

If you try to make everything in your life secure, what you gain in security you lose in freedom.

If you believe that you are of less value than other people and that you have no right to defend your own interests you will come to hate other people even more than you hate yourself.

If you believe that the way you see things is the only right way to see things and that anyone who disagrees with you is mad or bad, you will spend your life being angry, resentful, lonely and misunderstood.

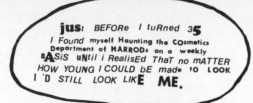

If you don't learn from your mistakes you are doomed to repeat them.

Or as my dad always said, 'You only get back what you give away.' So be sure you know what it is that you're giving away, because what affects you in the end is not what you give away, but how other people interpret what you're giving away.

The vultures come to rest in all kinds of places, not least in the furrows and wrinkles on your face as you get older. Your history gets written on your face. I'm not sure that pure thoughts and lots of moisturizer will ensure a beautiful ageing, but selfishness, anger, hatred, fear, bitterness, envy, jealousy and resentment will carve a monument to a wasted life.

CHAPTER 17

Living Your Own Life

WHAT OF the future?

Are our lives improving and will they get better and better? The economist Hamish McRae has considered these questions. He concludes his study of *The World in 2020* with:

> If we as individuals make sensible and humane decisions in the way we live our daily lives, then the societies in which we live will become more sensible and humane. More than this, the developed world will become a better model for those other countries which will achieve developed status. If on the other hand we are lazy, corrupt and greedy, then the rich world will not just lose influence; it will, in any meaningful sense of the word, become less rich. This is an issue for all people, not just for politicians. The more we can understand about the way the world is changing in the run up to 2020, the greater the chance we have of securing its future in the years beyond.[27]

Hamish McRae, being an economist, studied the economic and political issues which might determine our future, but he concluded that, 'Enduring prosperity requires societies which are stable, ordered and honest . . . Put bluntly, if countries wish to continue becoming richer, their people will have to learn to behave better.'[28]

Just how might this improvement in our behaviour come about?

Hamish McRae has no ready answer. He wonders whether

there might need to be some kind of fundamentalist revolution in the west, 'a grass-roots movement where ordinary people revived their faith in the Protestant ethic of honesty, hard work and family values', but he immediately sees that 'it could be destructive: one or more populist leaders encouraging the persecution of "deviants", meaning anyone who did not conform to the majority's idea of proper behaviour.'[29]

How could this fundamentalist revolution come about? How could we all, diverse as we are, become devoted to hard work or even agree on what we call honesty and family values? Am I, a single mum, devoid of family values?

Hamish McRae says, 'The most helpful guide to the way societies behave under pressure is their past.'[30] He does not specify which bit of the past. The wealth of Britain was built on the hard work of establishing and running the slave trade, but even the Tory Genghis Khans have not suggested a return to that (at least not in public). Unfortunately, Hamish McRae does not see that out of the wide array of ideas from which we can choose to help us decide how to live our lives we select those which seem to work. The idea called 'the Protestant ethic' worked in the nineteenth century for many people in the UK because there were plenty of jobs to be had. Those who couldn't get a job could try their luck in the USA or the colonies. However, in the later half of the twentieth century the Protestant ethic of hard work, honesty and family values, admirable though this ethic may be, will not secure for many millions of people their basic need to survive not just as a body but as a person. How can you work hard when there is no work to be had?

Many people, as Hamish McRae expounds, 'rob people in the streets, have children they cannot look after, waste the time of the courts by suing on absurd pretexts, drive dangerously, take drugs, fiddle their taxes or claim social security benefits to which they are not entitled'[31] and thus undermine the country's wealth. (Curiously, he does not mention greedy company directors, dishonest politicians and criminal tycoons.) He does not observe that the people he condemns interpret the crabbed and mean range of possibilities their society offers in such a way that what they do allows them to assert, 'I am I, and my existence has significance to me if to no one else.' Offered a better array of possibilities most of these people would more likely make 'sensible and humane decisions'.

Most historians would be surprised at the generality of his claim that 'the best guide (to what will happen) is history'.[32] Many other people have observed that all we can learn from history is that we don't learn from history. Every generation repeats the errors of all preceding generations.

Hamish McRae, as I know from my regular reading of his column in the *Independent*, is a humane, sensible, intelligent, educated man, and, like most other people similar to him, he does not understand how he and other people operate every moment of their lives. All his erudition and careful thought have no firm foundation for he does not understand that what people do, either as individuals or societies, in any field of activity, depends not on events but on how they interpret events, and while within groups there are shared interpretations no two people interpret events in exactly the same way.

Because we don't understand ourselves we have, generation after generation, inflicted suffering on others and on ourselves. It doesn't matter what great technological advances or scientific discoveries are made, if we cannot learn to understand ourselves and so end the suffering we both inflict and suffer, we show ourselves to be more stupid than the animals we despise. Dinosaurs lasted for four million years. Crocodiles and sharks have already lasted for longer than we ever will because our planet cannot sustain for ever our way of living.

Much of our suffering is a result of violence, the incidence of which has never decreased and which this century has increased. Kind, intellectual men like Hamish McRae deplore violence. Other equally kind, intellectual men are fascinated by violence.

The novelist Martin Amis, writing about violence and the video nasty *Child's Play 3* featuring the animated, vicious doll Chucky, wrote, 'Fairly representatively, I think, I happen to like screen violence while deploring its real life counterpart.' Having watched the video he concluded, 'I felt no urge or prompting to go out and kill someone.' However, 'what we have to imagine is a mind that, on exposure to Chucky, is already brimful of

post-Duchamp, anything tHE aRTist SelecTs iS art. the FAcT thaT mY selecTion consists Of eXhibiTions Of thE entrails OF Dismembered Animals in formaldehyde HaS nothing whAtever to do wiTh tHe number of violenTcarToons I waTched as a cHild. On the ConTrAry, iT belongs To The life affirming, caThartic, Dionysian TraditION thAt hAs ALWaYs been pARt of Art and its' Objects.

Chucky and things like Chucky. Then, if you mix in psychopath-
ology, stupidity, moral deformation, dreams of omnipotence
and sadism, and whatever else, Chucky is unlikely to affect anything but the *style* of your subsequent atrocities. Murderers have
to have something to haunt them: they need their internal pan-
demonium.'[33]

Martin Amis wrote this article for the *New Yorker* and it was
reprinted in the *Observer*. He is considered by many people to be
one of the outstanding thinkers of his generation. He explained
violence by listing the contents of the murderer's mind. This
list is a heterogeneous collection of ideas of varying degrees of
abstraction, reminiscent of a certain Chinese encyclopedia which
so enchanted Jorge Luis Borges and Michel Foucault by catego-
rizing animals as

(a) belonging to the Emperor, (b) embalmed, (c) tame,
(d) sucking pigs, (e) sirens, (f) fabulous, (g) stray dogs,
(h) included in the present classification, (i) frenzied, (j)
innumerable, (k) drawn with a fine camelhair brush, (l) et
cetera, (m) having just broken the water pitcher, (n) that
from a long way off look like flies.[34]

What Martin Amis here is demonstrating in his article is not
an understanding of the way we think and act but merely the
nonchalance which shows to his readers that he has passed the
rite of passage most boys pass so that other males will approve
of them. The rite is that they must see and perhaps interact with
something which is horrifying, vile and frightening. The test
is that they should show no emotion other than pleasurable
excitement. Nowadays video nasties provide that rite of passage
for many boys. What the rite produces in the boy is not the
inner strength which comes with self-understanding but an
insensitivity to others' pain and suffering and to the ugliness
which such insensitivity creates. (The ugliness of our urban
landscapes and the inhumanity of much of our architecture are
a result of such rites of passage.)

Martin Amis shows that he does not understand that the
effect a video nasty might have on a person depends on how

that person has interpreted it. Some people interpret such a video as giving them permission to behave likewise. Some people interpret the video as revealing something about the makers of the video, something which these viewers deplore and reject. For others the attraction of violence in films and videos arises from the discontent they feel with themselves and their lives.

Usually this discontent is a vague, unarticulated but pervasive feeling of having missed out on something and of being in some way flawed and misplaced, yet in another way whole and having been cheated out of a rightful place.

This vague feeling is their truth which they do not acknowledge, much less understand. There is a sense of rightness with which they were born, the memory of the denigration they suffered in childhood, leaving them with a sense of missing out on what they could have been and could have done. Rather than acknowledge their feelings and make their journey back into themselves to discover their original rightness, they prefer to see themselves as onlookers rather than someone who engages with life and all the uncertainty that entails. Sex and violence on film and video gives them the illusion of living without actually having to live.

Living, really living, is an exciting, chancy business.

You recognize how little you control in your life, but you see this not as something to fear but something to enjoy, for everything new is another opportunity.

You know that the world is not the way it seems, and that it certainly isn't the way it is supposed to be, but, rather than responding to this with fear or resentment, you enjoy testing out your interpretations, comparing them with other people's and looking for contrary evidence because such a way of living is sane, intelligent and interesting.

You are a good person, not because you fear punishment and hope for a reward, but because to be good – that is, in Hamish McRae's words, humane and sensible – gives you pleasure.

Because you know yourself, you take responsibility for yourself, and thus you create a stable centre to a changing life in a changing world.

When others show you love and appreciation you are pleased, but a dearth of love and appreciation holds no terrors for you because you love and appreciate yourself.

You know that you are ordinary in the way that every person who has existed, does and will exist is ordinary, and that you are special because you are unique, just as everyone is unique.

Living like this you do not need the imminence of death to remind you of the importance of living in the present. Every day is as Dennis Potter described it in an interview a few weeks before his own death.

> The only thing you know for sure is the present tense and that nowness becomes so vivid to me that I'm almost serene. I can celebrate life. Below my window in Ross now the blossom is out. It's a plum tree, it looks like apple blossom but it's white, and looking at it through the window when I'm writing it is the whitest, frothiest, blossomest blossom that there ever could be. Things are both more trivial and more important than they ever were and the difference between the trivial and the important doesn't seem to matter, but the nowness of everything is absolutely wondrous.[35]

Living is both strange and ordinary. Of course it does seem that all that experience, all that knowledge which is uniquely yours and which is so extraordinary, so much the essence of being alive, should be preserved for its sheer especialness in order that others can witness it and absorb into their lives your astounding, unique essence of being. However, the best you can hope for is that those who have known you will remember you with affection. Wanting your experience to be preserved forever is but a cry into the winds of time. Nothing of our experiences can be preserved for ever. A few meagre extracts can be kept in libraries and museums, but books, film and computer tapes decay, and the language and artistic forms which describe our experiences soon become archaic to those who follow us.

So what you must do is be aware that you are alive and what

you are creating as you encounter the world is yours, unique and special. Know it fiercely, sharply, without compromise and with a huge enjoyment of living, even though your living encompasses pain, loss and loneliness as well as love, closeness, contentment and joy. Pain and joy are all part of living.

You have a choice. You can exist. Or you can live.

CHAPTER 18

If You Want to Learn More

WHILE READING *The Guide* you might be thinking

'How does she know this?'

or

'It's all very well for Dorothy Rowe recommend that I change my interpretations but she doesn't say much about how to do this.'

or even

'I'd like to know more about this.'

Answers to all these can be found in my other books. In them are accounts of how I arrived at my conclusions, suggestions about how to change and much more information about each of the topics mentioned in *The Guide*.

My books don't have to be read in any particular order but here I shall describe them in chronological order so as to show not just what they are about but how my thinking has developed over the years.

Choosing Not Losing (HarperCollins 1978)

In 1971 I went to Lincolnshire to start and head the Department of Clinical Psychology for Lincolnshire. The Trent Regional Health Authority gave me a research grant but I soon discovered that my results could not be contained in the usual academic papers. So I wrote a book and my colleague Don Bannister put me in touch with Michael Coombes, the Psychology Editor of

John Wiley and Sons, who decided to publish the book with the title *The Experience of Depression*.

I had started doing research into depression when I arrived in England in 1968 and had written about this research in my PhD thesis and in a number of academic papers. I had tried to rid my prose of the psychological jargon academia requires (viz, never use a short word when a long one will do) but I still clung to the structure of an academic paper. Hence the chapters are organized in the order of theory, research design and results, discussion and conclusion.

Since 1968 I had read everything I could find about depression written by psychiatrists and psychoanalysts. (Psychologists back then weren't interested in depression.) Such writings were full of theory and patronizing and derogatory descriptions of people unfortunate enough to be patients but nowhere was there a description of the actual experience of depression. I found that in literature and biography and in what my patients told me.

I realized that the essence of the experience of depression was the sense of isolation, of being in a prison. I recognized these descriptions because in my final year at school and again when my marriage broke up there were times when I felt unable and unwilling to make the effort to be in close contact with other people. I am often asked, 'Have you ever been depressed?' To the extent that most people go through short periods of depression when their lives are changing markedly I have, but, having seen people rendered helpless and suffering by the experience of depression, I cannot say, as some people do, 'I am (or was) a depressive.'

In *Choosing Not Losing* I wrote:

> In referring to a particular language structure as the building of a wall around oneself I am not merely using a metaphor to describe an abstract concept. While different people describe their experience of depression in different ways, there is one feature which they all share. Each person describes the experience as one of being enclosed. Some say it is like being in a dark prison cell, some say it is like

being at the bottom of a deep hole, some say it is like being wrapped in an impenetrable cloth, some say it is being unable to move in the middle of a vast and empty desert, some say it is like being enclosed in thick, soundproofed glass. The images vary, but the underlying concept is the same. The person is in solitary confinement. And as the days pass, the torture grows worse. [p.50]

For me an important part of this book was in setting out for the first time my understanding of how we are in essence meaning-creating creatures. In each book I have tried another way of describing this but never perfectly because we cannot distance ourselves from our meaning-creating process in order to examine it.

Then there are the nine people in the book who talked with me for many months, even years. I came to know them very well.

The Courage to Live (HarperCollins 1982)

This book was first published by John Wiley and Sons under the title *The Construction of Life and Death*. I like that title but my new publishers HarperCollins thought differently.

This book has a simple thesis. Religious or not, everyone has a set of metaphysical beliefs, that is, meanings given to the nature of death and the purpose of life. I talked to people who coped with life and people who didn't, and I found that, whatever the nature of the beliefs each person held, those who coped with life had a set of beliefs which gave them courage and optimism and those who didn't cope had a set of beliefs which made them fearful and pessimistic.

I enjoyed myself reading philosophy and theology in researching for this book. By then I had also worked out a way of interweaving stories about the lives of people I had met with stories from my reading. However, I still wanted to show how our constructions of meaning reveal themselves in our conversation, and so a number of conversations are included in the book.

This book is the first to mention my research, which showed that the process of questioning to seek the reasons behind the reasons ended not with an ultimate reason which was unique to each person (which is what I expected to find) but ended in only one of two reasons. The human species has two sexes and two 'verts', introverts and extraverts. It was Peter in this book who enabled me to understand how an extravert experiences his/her sense of existence. If you're an introvert like me and you don't understand what extraverts mean when they say, 'I feel I don't exist,' or 'I'm frightened I'll disappear' read what Peter had to tell me (pp.224–228).

I ended this book by talking about how, if we want to be creative, we need to have in our meaning structure some random element.

> The random element in our construct system can be the decision to let things take their course, to see what turns up. It can also be the recognition of the mystery, the unknown, and the decision to open oneself to the possibility of contact with it. Contact, not control. Control of the mystery is magic, the attempt to bring the mystery within the narrow confines of our imagination. Magic tries to determine the outcome (and praying to God for gifts in return for good behaviour is a form of magic); mystery inspires the wonder and the terror of the unknown and the unknowable.
>
> Contact with the mystery is not just some great and rare experience. It is present when we feel ourselves most alive, when we are suffused with wonder, curiosity, surprise, or laughter. When we are most alive we are hopeful, and hope is only possible when there is uncertainty. To be certain is to be hopeless. [p.294]

Depression: The Way Out of Your Prison (Routledge 1983)

By 1981 I had been lecturing about depression quite frequently to professional groups. That year I was asked by a group in

Lincoln who were interested in all forms of alternative medicine to give an evening public lecture. That afternoon I put some notes for my talk on one side of a white card and duly gave my talk. The next day I happened to call at the natural health shop near Lincoln market to make a purchase of something healthy. There the manager asked me if the lecture I had given the previous night was contained in a book. If so, he was sure he could sell such a book.

I told him no, but as I walked up the street I realized that my notes for the lecture formed the outline of a book which I then set about writing. The book was for all those people who were like my patients, people who were not intellectuals or, in many cases, not particularly well educated, but who were being ground down by a misery they couldn't understand. I knew that I needed to find a publisher of popular books.

I had a tenuous connection with David Godwin (I can't remember what) when he was psychology editor at Routledge. David told me that he would be pleased to look at my manuscript, so I sent it. He then asked Leonie Caldicott, who had some knowledge of depression, to read it. Leonie told David that the book was worth publishing. So it was published by Routledge in 1983. In 1984 it won the MIND Book of the Year Award where, as a special bonus, I met Fay Weldon, one of the judges, and we became good friends.

When I had planned my public lecture on depression what I had scribbled on the white card was a list of six Real, Absolute and Immutable Truths. Believe these and you're depressed. In *Choosing Not Losing* I had listed many such Truths told to me by my depressed patients. By 1981 I had realized that such Truths, however expressed, could be grouped under six headings which form the recipe for depression. Here they are.

1. No matter how good and nice I appear to be, I am really bad, evil, valueless, unacceptable to myself and other people.
2. Other people are such that I must fear, hate and envy them.
3. Life is terrible and death is worse.

4. Only bad things happened to me in the past and only bad things will happen to me in the future.
5. It is wrong to get angry.
6. I must never forgive anyone, least of all myself. [p.15]

As I knew from my conversations with depressed people, what keeps people holding on to these Truths and thus on to their depression is pride.

If we want to live life fully we must have freedom, love and hope. So life must be an uncertain business. This is what makes it worthwhile.

But you want absolute certainty and you have too much pride to admit that you are wrong. You take pride in seeing yourself as essentially bad; you take pride in not loving and accepting other people; pride in the starkness and harshness of your philosophy of life; pride in the sorrows of your past and the blackness of your future; pride in recognizing the evil of anger; pride in not forgiving; pride in your high standards; pride in your sensitivity; pride in your refusal to lose face by being rejected; pride in your pessimism; pride in your martyrdom; pride in your suffering.

Pride, so Christian theology teaches, is the deadliest of the seven sins since it prevents the person from recognizing his sins and repenting and reforming. Sin or not, it is pride that keeps you locked in the prison of depression. It is pride which prevents you from changing and finding your way out of the prison. [p.128]

Giving up these beliefs and the pride you take in them can be difficult, especially if your loved ones don't want you to change in any fundamental way. So I included in this book many suggestions about how to change.

Living with the Bomb: Can We Live Without Enemies?
(Routledge 1985)

David Godwin left Routledge and my new editor was Stratford
Caldicott. These were the years when the threat of nuclear war
was at its height. Over lunch one day Stratford and I were
discussing this and I remarked, 'War has always been inevitable.
The way we bring up our children and organize our society
makes enemies necessary.' Stratford asked, 'How do you work
that out?' I told him. Stratford said, 'Why don't you write a
book about it?' So I did.

Living with the Bomb: Can We Live Without Enemies? was
published in 1985. It is the least successful of my books. As I
discovered from all the lectures I gave and the conferences I
attended, some people (mainly women) in the Campaign for
Nuclear Disarmament and other anti-nuclear groups were interested in what I had to say but the men of the anti-nuclear
movements, many of these public figures involved in politics,
science and academia, did not even want to acknowledge
the question, much less discuss 'Can we live without
enemies?'

When I wrote this book I was well aware that the threat of
the nuclear bomb was not our only worry. There were other
bombs, what I called

> **The Debt Bomb**, which can destroy all the major
> systems of commerce and trading on which we depend (to
> which I would now add the vast international derivatives
> market, little regulated and little understood by those
> whose job it is to know).

> **The Population Bomb**, which means too many people
> competing for the world's resources and many suffering
> irreparable mental and physical damage through starvation.

> **The Ecology Bomb**, which will make the planet unin-
> habitable by humans. [p.193]

These 'bombs' are derived from how we organize our groups. The late historian E. P. Thompson said in a lecture which the BBC refused to broadcast:

> There appears to be a universal need for 'the Other' as a means of defining the identity of any group, and of the individuals within it. We cannot define who 'we' are without defining the identity of any group, and of the individuals within it. We cannot define who 'we' are without defining 'them' – those who are not 'us'. If 'they' can be seen as threatening, then our own bonding and self identity are all the stronger. Rome required barbarians. Christendom required pagans or heathens, Protestant and Catholic Europe required each other. The nation state bonded itself against other nations. The same process may be followed in the family, community, and in sects; and also in class formation. [p.146]

To survive we have to live in groups. We define our group in terms of those who are excluded – the Outsider or the Stranger. The Stranger provides the solution to the problem of what to do with our aggression which would disrupt the group. This aggression is partly our natural aggression and partly the anger and self-hate we acquire when, as children, we are taught to be good. We project much of this aggression, anger and hate on to the Stranger. Thus we can say to ourselves, 'I might not be very valuable but I belong to the best group in the world. We are all clean, unselfish, responsible and unaggressive. Our enemies are dirty, selfish, greedy, irresponsible and aggressive.'
Enemies wouldn't be necessary if we understood ourselves.

Beyond Fear (HarperCollins 1987)

Walter Swartz of the *Guardian* wrote an article about *Living with the Bomb* and for this Don McPhee took an extraordinary photograph of me at RAF Waddington standing (illegally) with a Vulcan bomber looming over me. Every hour of the day and night one of these bombers, carrying nuclear bombs, patrolled the skies. RAF Waddington was next door to St John's Psychiatric Hospital where the patients could watch the Vulcans taking off and landing and wonder who it was that was crazy.

Impressed by the photograph and/or Walter's article, Mike Fishwick, then editor of Fontana at Collins (now Harper-Collins) got in touch with my agent Imogen Parker and made an offer for my next book which Imogen and I felt we could not refuse. Mike and I met and so began a great relationship. Mike thinks I'm wonderful and everything I write is wonderful (or so he says), he always hurries to resolve my every concern, he is marvellously teasable and he makes me laugh. What else could a writer possibly wish for?

By the mid-eighties the Conservative government's plans to turn the National Health Service into a business were well under way. Ever since I had first set foot in a psychiatric hospital (in 1949 in Concord Hospital, Sydney, where I saw a small, elderly man given electroconvulsive therapy without an anaesthetic. It took six young men to hold his wrenching, twisting body on the table) I had been appalled and angered by the cruelty of the psychiatric system which presented itself in the guise of doing good. To this was now added the ideas of a group of politicians who, in the words of that old saying, knew the price of everything and the value of nothing.

I was well aware that the psychiatric system, while purporting to care for the individual, actually functions as an arm of the State, charged, like the police, with keeping order. Trying to meet such a system head-on would be wasted effort. Far more effective would be to circumvent it by speaking directly to the people who were or might be in its clutches and give them the information they needed to sort out their lives. I began this campaign with *Depression: The Way Out of Your Prison* and followed it with *Beyond Fear*.

This book is about fear and our defences against fear.

Fear is too fearful to be discussed. We talk about what we do to protect ourselves against this fear – we worry about practical things or unlikely eventualities, or we work hard, or become bad tempered or extremely powerful, or we cling tenaciously to some religious or political faith, or we drink too much, or become ill, or depressed, and so on – but we do not talk about the total, annihilating terror we feel when we as much as glimpse our own insignificance, vulnerability, helplessness, isolation, weakness and fragility in this limitless, incomprehensible cosmos. We fear death, but far worse than death is the annihilation of our self. [p.11]

Annihilation of the self is our greatest fear. It is worse than bodily death, for after death we can imagine our self, or some important aspect of our self, our children, our work, the remembrances of friends, continuing on, but after annihilation there is nothing of our self to carry on. We have gone, brushed aside like chalk off a blackboard, engulfed like a raindrop in an ocean, consumed like a dead leaf on a fire, swirled away like a puff of smoke when the wind blows. After annihilation our body may continue to function but that which was our self has gone. [p.49]

We can feel the threat of such annihilation whenever we discover that we have misinterpreted events. If we have confidence in ourselves we have confidence in our ability to put right any such misinterpretations. If we have little confidence in ourselves the slightest error fills us with fear.

Beyond Fear shows how, as we lose more and more self-confidence, the more extreme become the defences we use against this fear of annihilation. At first the defences are no more than regular habits, such as organizing chaos by writing a list. Then they become oddities of behaviour, and finally the defences which psychiatrists call mental illnesses.

Which defences we choose to use depends not just on our degree of self-confidence but on how we perceive the threat of annihilation. Some of us (those I call extraverts) see this threat as being complete rejection and abandonment. For the rest of us (those I call introverts) the threat is that of falling into chaos. Under the extremes of threat extraverts defend with phobias and, failing that, mania. Introverts defend with obsessions and compulsions and, failing that, schizophrenia. Depression is a defence available to us all.

What renders such defences unnecessary is to accept and value yourself.

The Successful Self (HarperCollins 1988)

By the time *Beyond Fear* was published I had left the National Health Service. Now I had time to write, not just about our fear of annihilation, but about something much more positive, how we experienced our sense of self. I wrote,

> Now I am fifty-six I know why some of us stand hesitant to act upon the world and remain inside the only security they know, and why others of us scurry around in the hard brightness of the world, fearing and denying the darkness within. I also know why some of us go forth confidently. These are the people who have confronted their own unreal reality. If the world outside them seemed unreal, they acted as if it was real, and, lo, it became real. If the reality within themselves was dense and dark, they journeyed into it and made it light. They took their little, frightened self, standing hesitant upon the threshold of an unreal reality and made the unreal real. Thus they created for themselves The Successful Self.
>
> Such people lead successful lives. This does not necessarily mean that they are successful in terms of fame, wealth and power, though many are, but that they are successful in terms of their own values and aims. Given that life is a chancy business, they are secure, and given that relationships are always complicated, they live comfortably with themselves and others.
>
> Real success, that success which does not turn eventually into emptiness and lonely bitterness, is based upon the creation of the Successful Self. Such a creation is possible for all of us. [p.16]

So I travelled the world talking to people who showed the signs of being Successful Selves. They had learned how to do what their way of experiencing their sense of existence hadn't taught them to do.

Extraverts, unless handicapped by a marked lack of self-confidence, have no difficulty in making and maintaining relationships. To be Successful Selves they need to learn two things:

1. It isn't frightening and forbidden to explore your internal reality. Rather it is interesting and very important to do so.
2. If you are completely on your own you don't disappear.

Introverts, unless handicapped by a marked lack of self-confidence, have no difficulty in creating order and imposing that order on the chaos around them. To be a Successful Self they need to learn

1. The simple social skills that establish and maintain relationships.
2. That everything that exists is in constant change, that all imposed order is temporary and often an illusion, and that what they call chaos is also freedom.

In *The Successful Self* I examined some of the many differing ways extraverts and introverts think, feel and behave in the same situation and how, in the way that opposites attract, extraverts and introverts are drawn together to form couples, and then fight one another because they each have different priorities.

It is by discovering the self-confidence with which we were born and by learning what we need to learn we are able to achieve

> our own individual synthesis of being an introvert and an extravert. Of course, as a born extravert we keep looking around for some extra stimulation, and as a born introvert we keep organizing, but, tolerating our long established

idiosyncrasies, we achieve not merely the idealized notion of being both an individual and a close-knit member of a group, but the real, lived experience of being one's unique self and an integral part of the continuous and continual life of the planet, as much a part of life as a wave is part of the ocean. [p.280]

Breaking the Bonds (HarperCollins 1991)
also *Breaking the Bonds Audiobook* (HarperCollins 1992)

If you have a large black-covered book called *The Depression Handbook* cherish it because it is a rare volume, the hardback version of *Breaking the Bonds*. HarperCollins marketing thought that *The Depression Handbook* was not a sufficiently upbeat title and so the paperback bore the title *Breaking the Bonds*.

I knew that for a great many people *Depression: The Way Out of Your Prison* was a way of understanding depression which gave them hope and helped them through their darkest time. Many people have said to me, 'That book saved my life.' However, I knew there was a gap in that book's explanation of why, at a particular time, a person selected from an array of possible interpretations that set of interpretations which created the prison of depression.

I wanted to fill in this gap. I also wanted to set down an account of what prevented people from changing and what they could do if they wanted to change. The debate about whether depression was a physical illness and whether drugs cured depression was still dragging on, and I wanted to write about this and about the jargon which professionals used. So I decided to write another book about depression, a sort of 'all you wanted to know about depression but were too depressed to ask' book.

My friend Ron Janoff suggested that I take as a basis for the book the search many people undertake in order to find out about depression and to address the book to those people who are depressed, or who have someone they care about who is depressed, or who at work have to deal with people who are depressed.

Thus I began the book by describing how you might set about trying to discover all you could about depression – reading books, talking to psychiatrists, therapists, even clergy. I well knew what is always the result of such a search.

So, whatever you have done to try to discover what depression is and how you might bring it to an end, all that has happened is that you have become more and more confused, and when we are confused we feel powerless and helpless.

The aim of this book is to help you sort out your confusion and regain that which is rightly yours, the power to understand yourself and the society in which you live, so that you can make the best decisions about how you should live your life. With such power we can not only understand the causes and the purposes of depression but, more importantly, free ourselves from its prison and live life joyfully, hopefully and freely.

To do this, we begin by understanding our own, lived experience.

It is our own real, lived experience which leads us into the prison of depression. It is not a gene, or our hormones, or our dysfunctional and illogical thinking, our lack of faith, or our complexes and inadequacies which have brought depression upon us, it is what has happened to us and, most importantly, what we have made of what happened to us; it is the conclusions we drew from our experience.

That set of conclusions which leads us, finally, into the prison of depression was not drawn illogically, or fantastically, or crazily, but were the correct conclusions to draw, given the information we had at the time.

If, when you were a child, all the adults you loved and trusted were telling you that you were bad and if you didn't mend your ways terrible things would happen to you, you wisely and correctly drew the conclusion that you were bad and had to work hard to be good. If, when you were a child, all the people you loved and trusted left you or disappointed or betrayed you, you wisely and correctly drew the conclusion that you must be wary of other people and that you should never love anyone completely ever again. You were not to know that if we grow up believing that we are intrinsically bad, and that other people are dangerous, we shall become increasingly isolated, the joy will disappear from our life, and that we shall fall into despair. Even if you did know that, you had to protect yourself. We all have to protect ourselves when we are in danger. The business of life is to live, and this is what we all try to do. [p.xix]

My way of sorting out such confusion was, first, to set out how we lay the basis for a later depression and why this happens. Next I examined why it is so hard to change. It is not just that depression is a defence. Other people try to stop us from changing.

Changing I described as a journey, and here I wrote in some detail about what we need to find along the way. This and both preceding sections are linked to a section called 'Discoveries' where I suggest a number of ways whereby you can examine your own meaning structure.

The final section, 'Technical Footnotes' covers matters such as why it is so important to psychiatrists to say that depression is a physical illness, and the effects of drugs, therapy and jargon. Then there is journey's end.

When you come to the end of your journey you will find, as you have always known, that you are you, and in yourself and in the world, you are at home. [p.302]

Wanting Everything (HarperCollins 1991)

This book examines a question I had been puzzling over ever since I was a small child: *Why can't people see what the effects of their actions are going to be?*

My mother was a very intelligent woman. Much of her bitterness stemmed from the fact that she had been denied the opportunity to use her intelligence. Yet in her dealings with other people, especially her nearest and dearest, she made mistake after mistake. She never seemed to learn from her mistakes, or at least not until she was very old. If, at my birth, she had decided to convince me that she did not love me and was ashamed of me, and to make sure I went right away from her emotionally and later physically, she could not have done a better job than she did. Yet actually what she wanted was for me to love her, to stay close to her and look after her as she had looked after her mother. Why was she so stupid?

I began learning about history and politics while I was in infants school and my father would talk to me about the civil war in Spain that was then raging. I became passionately interested in history, and yet all the time I was puzzled as to why all these great leaders could not see the inevitable outcome of their actions. Why didn't they realize that in a war *everybody* suffers, the victors as well as the vanquished? How could they not realize that if you treat people badly they will resent you and seek every occasion to do you down? Why were they so stupid?

I became a psychologist and found such stupidity rampant in my profession and in psychiatry. Fancy expecting people to get better when you herd them together in locked wards and treat them as the lowest of the low? Didn't they know that when they assessed a 'patient' or a 'subject' that person is busy assessing them and that that assessment is a powerful factor in the situation? How could they be so stupid?

We call ourselves *homo sapiens* but the *sapiens* relates only to our ability to understand inanimate objects. In understanding ourselves we are very stupid.

This isn't an innate stupidity. We're all born with the ability to empathize, that is, understand about other people. Tragically, our education takes that away from us.

Just how this happens, and why, I set out in *Wanting Everything*. We come into the world wanting everything and believing we can get it because in the womb to want was to get. We are told by the adults around us we can't have everything but because they bamboozle us with their explanations we don't realize that by relinquishing the 'everything' of the womb we can get everything in life that is really worth having. Instead, uncomprehendingly, we continue to try to get the first 'everything'. We try various strategies which I describe but inevitably we fail. I explain why.

Yet there was always an alternative.

If, thousands of years ago, we had realized that we needed to understand what we did to one another and why, we would not have been able to eradicate from our lives death and the loss of love, but we would have been able to find ways of supporting one another in times of suffering, because we would have been kinder to and more tolerant of one another. We would have turned our attention to unravelling the complex network of human interactions, and today would have developed a science of psychology as profound and complex as that of nuclear physics: not a science understood by an elite few, but one understood by everybody; a science not separate from daily life, but one which is an integral part of how we live, informing our choices and offering consolation for our failures and defeats. . . .

If, thousands of years ago, we had decided to use our intelligence to understand ourselves, we would have understood our wanting everything and have dealt with it, not by denial and blind grasping, but by turning 'everything' from the demand for immediate gratification into enlightened self-interest. We would have understood and taught our children that we should practise kindness, tolerance and sharing, not because they will assure our place in heaven or because they are the Great Virtues, but because a society where all the people practise kindness, tolerance and sharing is a pleasant place to live. It is in our own interests that we be kind, tolerant and share with others. We would have understood and taught our children that, since our life is limited, we have to make choices and order priorities, and, since we cannot have everything, we should focus on having the best. We would have understood and taught our children that a close and loving relationship gives more peace and joy and satisfaction than luxury and wealth, and that the capacity to live in the present and feel joined to and enthused by a vision of nature or a work of art gives more of a sense of being alive and excited and satisfied than the power of exploiting other people. We would have understood and taught our children that only by being responsible for ourselves can we be responsible for other people. We would have understood and taught our children that self-sacrifice is waste and that revenge, except in terms of mutual merriment, is futile.

If, thousands of years ago, we had decided to use our intelligence, how very different our lives would have been! [pp.359–361]

Time on Our Side (HarperCollins 1994)

When my agent Imogen Parker first suggested that I do a book on how we feel about time passing and growing older I was in the midst of writing *Wanting Everything* and wasn't thinking about time and age. However, I soon began to do so.

In 1990 I turned sixty and although I didn't feel any older I became increasingly aware that there were many people who thought I had reached my dotage. Moreover, the economic and political changes of the Eighties had caused many able people to discover that as far as the job market was concerned they were too old to work. At thirty-nine you could be a rising young executive and at forty a has-been. In addition, whenever I went to Australia I visited my two surviving aunts, each of whom was in a nursing home. One aunt was in a home where she was treated with dignity and respect, but the other aunt was in a nursing home where the patients were fed, watered, washed and treated as imbeciles for whom dignity and respect were quite unnecessary. Now time and age seemed to be especially important for me.

We fear getting older, yet most of our fears are unnecessary since we could ameliorate all the inevitable aspects of ageing.

Our fear grows out of the history of our species where the old have always mistreated the young. Researching and writing about the history of childhood I found very painful. It was not surprising that there was and is a mutual antipathy between the young and the old. Given our lack of understanding of ourselves, it was not surprising that in middle age we start to see and to fear the consequences of our actions in earlier decades.

However, we can become wise. We can learn that

We are totally responsible for ourselves. We can never be totally responsible for other people because we cannot be in control of everything which might affect them, and we can never control how other people interpret what happens to them. We cannot control most of what happens to us, but we do control how we interpret what happens to us. We can choose from a multitude of meanings. Thus we are totally responsible for how we interpret what happens to us, but, whatever interpretations we choose to make, certain consequences will follow.

Choose to fear time passing and growing old, and certain consequences will follow. You'll feel trapped and, one way or another, you will be unhappy.

Choose to see that the nature of life is change, and that to deny that everything changes, and to try to keep everything the same is to suffer, then other consequences follow. You will be free, and you will have a good chance of being happy.

'Suffering,' so the Buddhists tell us, 'is the attempt to make reality repeatable.'

Perhaps there should be two words for suffering – the suffering others inflict on us, and the suffering we inflict on ourselves.

We cause ourselves to suffer when we fail to understand that the nature of life is change, and that the nature of human beings is to create and impose meaning on the everchanging interconnectedness of everything that exists.

We suffer when we fail to understand that time, like

everything else we know, is a meaning which we have constructed.

However, everything that exists is not just a collection of our own individual meanings. There are real events (physical reality and other people's meanings) and our task should be to get as close as we can to understanding what reality is, even though we can never know it directly. If we do not constantly try to do this we become lost in our own idiosyncratic and increasingly unreal world.

To approximate reality we need to be able to compare our approximations of reality with those of other people. If we base our lives on the principle 'All the world's mad except me and thee, and even thee's a little mad' we cannot carry out the reality-testing operations which enable us to make sound judgements about reality, and so respond to our perceptions of reality in ways which advance our interests. We need to develop an understanding of other people and of ourselves which allows us to be unafraid of being close to other people. If, when young, you hate the old, and, when old, you hate the young, you will go through life being unable to approximate reality to the degree you need to achieve in order to live safely, wisely and happily. [pp.356–7]

Many of my readers write or talk to me about the books of mine they've read. A few people who are offended when I say that depression is not a physical illness or that beating children is unwise write to tell me how wrong I am. Most people tell me that they find my books helpful, and that is very pleasing because it is good to know that my private cogitations are not simply the workings of the intense internal reality of an introvert but have some relevance to other people's lives. It pleases me that something I do helps make other people happier. I know that my life is better when I'm surrounded by happy people rather than miserable, angry, bitter and often power-mad people.

Sometimes when I give a public talk people will ask me to sign copies of my books which they've owned for a long time.

These copies are dog-eared and well-read, often with passages underscored and annotated. This is especially pleasing to me because it shows that these books have become something lasting and important in the person's life.

At one bookshop where I was to speak I got into conversation with a woman as we each reached for an orange juice. We agreed that it was a pleasant evening, and then she said rather shyly, 'I'd like to tell you how I feel about your books. If I'm lonely I get out one of your books and read it. It's like having a friend to talk to.' What a wonderful thing to hear!

I hope you find my books to be good companions.

NOTES

1. Xenophanes, quoted by Karl R. Popper in 'On the Sources of Knowledge and Ignorance', *Proceedings of the British Academy*, Oxford University Press, London, 1960, p.66.
2. Albert Einstein, 'Geometry and Experience' in *Sidelights on Relativity*, trs G. B. Jeffrey and W. Perrett, Methuen & Co. Ltd, 1922, p.28.
3. Collins *Concise English Dictionary*, 1978.
4. Nigel Lewis, *The Book of Babel*, Viking, London, 1994, p.63.
5. Erwin Schrödinger, 'Mind and Matter' in *What Is Life?*, Cambridge University Press, 1993, p.93.
6. Dorothy Rowe, *The Courage to Live*, HarperCollins, 1989, p.225.
7. John Lennon, in his song 'Beautiful Boy', 1979.
8. Michael Leunig cartoon, *The Age*, 21 December 1991.
9. Fiona Buckland cartoon, 'Stark Reality', *Wanting Everything* p.327.
10. A. Moir, *Sydney Morning Herald*, 12 July 1994.
11. Cotham cartoon, *Bulletin of the Atomic Scientists*, August 1993, p.50.
12. Nigel Lewis, op. cit., p. 223.
13. John Gribbin, *In the Beginning: The Birth of the Living Universe*, Penguin, London, 1994, p.225.
14. King Fahd, *Observer*, 7 July 1990.
15. Vaclav Havel, *Letters to Olga*, tr. Paul Wilson, Faber, London, 1990, p.268.
16. Fiona Buckland, 'Born to Wash', *Wanting Everything* p.302.
17. Nigel Lewis, op. cit., p.3.
18. Ibid, p.10.
19. Sally Laird, *Observer*, 5 June 1994.
20. Michael Reddy, 'The Conduit Metaphor', in Andrew Ortony, ed., *Metaphor and Thought*, Cambridge University Press, Cambridge, 1979, pp.284–324.
21. Henry Beston, *The Outermost House*, Holt Rinehart Winston, 1928, quoted by Richard Ellis in *The Book of Sharks*, Alfred A Knopf, New York, 1989.
22. G. J. Whitrow, *The Natural Philosophy of Time*, Clarendon Press, Oxford, 1980, p.64.

23. Drennan cartoon, *Punch*, 13 May 1988.
24. *The Money Programme*, BBC TV, June 1994.
25. Pat McNeill cartoon, *Time on Our Side* p.214.
26. Julie Flint, *Observer*, 9 August, 1992.
27. Hamish McRae, *The World in 2020*, HarperCollins, 1994, p.277.
28. Ibid, p.264, 265.
29. Ibid, p.267.
30. Ibid, p.268.
31. Ibid, p.265.
32. Ibid, p.267.
33. Martin Amis, 'Acts of Violence', *Observer*, 3 July 1994.
34. Quoted in *The Order of Things*, Michel Foucault, Tavistock, London, 1970, p.xv.
35. Dennis Potter interview with Melvyn Bragg, *Without Walls*, Channel Four, 7 April 1994.

INDEX